# *The*
# PRICE *of* PEACE

## CAHAL B. DALY

D1470868

THE
**BLACKSTAFF PRESS**
BELFAST

First published in 1991 by
The Blackstaff Press Limited
3 Galway Park, Dundonald, Belfast BT16 0AN, Northern Ireland

Typeset by Textflow Services Limited

Printed by Billings and Sons Limited

British Library Cataloguing in Publication Data
Daly, Cahal B. (Cahal Brendan) *1917–*
The price of peace.
1. Northern Ireland. Conflict
I. Title
941.60824
ISBN 0-85640-471-3 (hardback)
0-85640-472-1 (paperback)

# CONTENTS

# PREFACE

This book is substantially based on addresses and homilies delivered during my last two years as Bishop of Ardagh and Clonmacnois and during my period as Bishop of Down and Connor, from 1982 to 1990. The content has been rearranged and revised, and considerable new material has been specially written for this publication.

The Second Vatican Council summoned the Church and specifically the bishops to be partisans of peace and workers for justice. The Decree on the Bishops' Pastoral Office in the Church (*Christus Dominus*) says:

> [Bishops] should set forth the ways by which are to be solved the very grave questions concerning the ownership, increase and just distribution of material goods, peace and war, and brotherly relations among all peoples . . . With a special concern they should attend upon the poor and the deprived, to whom the Lord sent them to preach the Gospel. [*Christus Dominus*, nos. 12–13]

The Pastoral Constitution on the Church in the Modern World (*Gaudium et Spes*) says:

> The Council wishes to recall first of all the permanent binding force of universal natural law and its all-embracing principles . . . Therefore, actions which deliberately conflict with these same principles, as well as orders commanding such actions, are criminal. Blind obedience cannot excuse those who yield to them . . .
>
> Peace is not merely absence of war . . . Instead it is rightly and properly called 'the effect of justice'. Peace is the fruit of the harmony built into human society by its divine founder, and is brought about by men and women as they strive to attain an even more perfect justice . . .
>
> Peace is not something that can ever be attained once and for all, but something that must be constantly built up . . . A peace of this kind cannot be obtained on earth unless the welfare of

individual persons is carefully protected and unless men and women are prepared freely and trustingly to share with each other the riches of their own minds as well as their talents. A firm determination to respect the dignity of other men and women and other peoples, as well as deliberate practice of fraternal love, are absolutely essential if peace is ever to be achieved. Hence peace is also the fruit of love, because love goes beyond what justice can provide. [*Gaudium et Spes*, no. 78]

Pope John Paul II, addressing the Catholic Bishops of Ireland in Dublin on 30 September 1979, said:

I earnestly hope that, in a continued effort, you and our brothers and sisters in the faith will become spokesmen for the just reasons of peace and reconciliation before those who wield the swords and those who perish by the sword . . . Venerable pastors of the Church in Ireland: this service to justice and social love that is yours to perform in this present moment is difficult. It is difficult, but it is your duty! Do not fear: Christ is with you! He will give you his Holy Spirit: the Spirit of counsel and fortitude. And although this Spirit of God is frequently resisted, in the heart of man and the history of humanity, by 'the spirit of this world' and by 'the spirit of darkness', nevertheless the final victory can only be that of love and truth . . . Be assured that in your ministry you have my support and that of the universal Church. And all men and women of good will stand by you in the quest for peace, justice and human dignity.

This book is the result of some efforts made over the past decade to contribute to that service to justice and social love of which the Holy Father spoke. The knowledge of the Holy Father's personal interest in our difficulties, his support and his constant prayer for us are an immense encouragement.

I have many people to thank for their help in preparing these texts for publication. I particularly thank my former student Mrs Gemma Loughran for her invaluable editorial work. I thank the Down and Connor Diocesan Office staff in Lisbreen, Belfast, for their dedicated and efficient services throughout the whole process.

This volume goes to the publishers as I leave the Diocese of Down and Connor for the Archdiocese of Armagh. I dedicate it to the Church of Down and Connor, which has come through a great tribulation and has not failed in the test of fidelity to the Lord and to His kingdom of justice, love and peace. I dedicate it to the priests of Down and Connor, who have stayed close to their people in days of trial and grief, planting love where many tried to sow hate, spreading forgiveness in place of bitterness, building peace in place of violence, inspiring hope instead of despair. I dedicate it to the religious sisters and brothers of Down and Connor, whose prayer and pastoral caring have helped to heal so many broken hearts and bruised people. I dedicate it to the laity of Down and Connor, who have by their praying and their Christian living served the Lord 'day and night in His sanctuary', the sanctuary of the churches, the sanctuary of their homes. They are 'the joy and the crown' of the priests and bishops of the diocese. They are the sign that love triumphs over every adversity 'in the power of Him who loved us' (Romans 8: 37).

# 1
## THE TWO TRADITIONS

*Each human community – ethnic, historical, cultural or reli-*
*gious – has rights which must be respected. Peace is threatened*
*every time one of these rights is violated . . . As long as injus-*
*tices exist in any of the areas that touch upon the dignity of*
*the human person, be it in the political, social or economic*
*field, be it in the cultural or religious sphere, true peace will*
*not exist. The causes of inequalities must be identified through*
*a courageous and objective evaluation, and they must be*
*eliminated, so that every person can develop and grow in*
*the full measure of his or her humanity.* [Pope John Paul II,
Address at Drogheda, 29 September 1979; in *The Pope in Ireland*, Veritas
Publications, Dublin, 1979, p. 24]

The heart of Northern Ireland's problem, both political and
moral, is the failure to recognise the civil and political rights of
the two historic traditions and communities here. It is, however, not enough to discern the 'two traditions'. It is a political
necessity and it is a moral obligation to accord full constitutional recognition to both identities and give proper political
and institutional expression, at all levels of decision-making, to
each.

THE NATURE OF THE TWO IDENTITIES

There are two quite distinct kinds of Ulster regional loyalty,
one which can meaningfully be called that of 'British Ulster',
and the other that of 'Irish Ulster'. There are two distinct
forms of 'Ulster identity', forms that are distinct historically,
culturally, socially and politically. Each group understands and
lives its Ulster identity, in all ways that are politically relevant,
quite differently from the other. There is, to repeat, an 'Irish
Ulster identity', and there is a 'British Ulster identity'.

The publicity of Sinn Féin and the Irish Republican Army
(IRA) talks of the 'British presence', the 'British occupation' of
the North of Ireland, as if this were something extraneous to

the Northern Ireland situation; something which could be ended unilaterally by Britain's simply withdrawing her army and her governmental institutions. This is to ignore the fact that there are in Northern Ireland roughly 1 million people – who have been on this island for more than three hundred years, and who form a rightful and permanent part of Irish reality – who owe allegiance to Britain; they profess a British identity, claim British citizenship, and demand the presence and protection of the British Army, which they see as 'their army'. These rightful inhabitants of this island of Ireland are a 'British presence' in Ireland. They are a 'British dimension' in Ireland. Indeed, in the most relevant sense of that term, they are *the* 'British presence' in Ireland.

In the words of the poet, John Hewitt, they can say:

> For we have rights drawn from the soil and sky;
> the use, the pace, the patient years of labour,
> the rain against the lips, the changing light,
> the heavy clay-sucked stride, have altered us;
> we would be strangers in the Capitol;
> this is our country also, no-where else;
> and we shall not be outcast on the world.
> [from 'The Colony', in *The Selected John Hewitt*, Blackstaff Press, 1981]

These unionists feel that they gained liberation and self-determination when the Northern state was set up; they see those values as diminished and threatened now; they currently view the republican physical force campaign as an attack upon their community and a threat to its rights and its freedoms and an attempt to coerce them into unwilling submission.

No future for Ireland is conceivable or could be just that does not take account of their feelings, that does not respect their rights, that does not offer hope of securing their consent. No talk of 'British withdrawal', from whatever source it comes, is either politically meaningful or morally admissible that does not take cognisance of the rightful presence in Ireland of this million people, and that does not provide a *modus convivendi*, acceptable to them as well as to the Northern minority, whereby the unionist and the nationalist communities can live together in mutual respect for one another's just rights. No political solution for Northern Ireland, no political blueprint for the future of the whole of Ireland, can be taken seriously that does not offer realistic hopes of securing agreement from the unionist population, and point to feasible ways of convincing them of the rightness and the value, for themselves too, of whatever settlement is proposed.

I have said that the so-called 'British dimension' is internal to Northern Ireland. But it is equally true that the 'Irish dimension' is internal to Northern Ireland. It is embodied in the hearts and minds of well over half a million Ulster people who are as much part of Northern Ireland as Ulster loyalists are. Their sense of Irishness is as rightful and as valid as is the loyalists' sense of Britishness. The vast majority of them totally reject violence as a way of advancing their Irish nationalist aims. Their tradition, their peaceful aspiration, are no threat to anyone. Their aspiration is peacefully and lawfully expressed; and it should be peacefully accepted and constitutionally recognised as part of what defines Northern Ireland. The expression of it is, indeed, a fundamental human right, and should be accepted as such.

In Northern Ireland each of our divided communities has had its own vision, pursued its own aspirations, to the exclusion of the other community's vision and aspirations; each has implicitly or overtly located its own utopia in a place free of the disturbing presence of the other. A united Irish nationalist Ireland with no British presence; a united British and unionist Ulster with no Irish or nationalist dimension – both visions have been pursued with fanatical dedication and often through the blood and tears of others down many decades of our history. One person's vision has been another's nightmare.

Northern Ireland's problem is that of how to find ways of sharing two traditions, not ways of suppressing one or other tradition, or of subordinating one to the other. It is a problem of giving political expression to two equally valid loyalties, which each have an equally valid historic and moral right to be, and to be constitutionally recognised as being, an integral part of

5

Northern Ireland. Recognition of two Ulster loyalties, two Ulster identities, is an indispensable precondition of any solution to the complex problems of Northern Ireland.

## Past constitutional arrangements

The tragedy of Northern Ireland is that it has never been given constitutional arrangements that are appropriate to the political composition of its population. Its unionist population is too large to be absorbed into a united Ireland conceived on unitary nationalist lines. Its nationalist population is too large to be absorbed into a Northern Ireland conceived on unitary unionist lines. It was, however, precisely a unitary and univocally unionist and British constitutional model that was devised for Northern Ireland at the creation of the state. This constitution was appropriate to the unionist part of its population, but by no means to its nationalist part.

Northern Ireland was defined as an integral and inseparable part of the United Kingdom (UK), and its citizenship was defined as British. This definition coincides exactly with the definition of the Union. This in turn coincides exactly with the statement of unionist political principles. This is a natural and just expression of unionist aspirations and a safeguard of the rights of the unionist part of the population. But it ignores completely the aspirations and the rights of the nationalist population, which is by definition non-unionist. Under the Northern Ireland constitution, nationalists could not, while remaining nationalists, give unqualified endorsement to the constitution, which was a British and unionist one. They could not hope to share in government unless they exchanged their nationalist convictions for unionist ones. It is a basic injustice in any country's constitution that it requires a citizen to change his or her political party before being allowed to share in the government of the state of which he or she is a citizen.

Historically, of course, the conception of the Northern Ireland state was based on the hypothesis that it would provide some form of power-sharing within the island of Ireland. In effect, the British government of the time opted for a territorial form of power-sharing, with unionists being given control over the northeast of the island, where a unionist majority was assured, and nationalists being given control over the rest of the island, where the nationalist majority was unquestionable. This could fairly be claimed to have been a well-intentioned compromise. It may have seemed to the British administration at that time to be the best, if not the only possible, solution to an intractable problem. It was, in any case, not intended to be a permanent, but only a provisional, solution. It is untrue and unjust to say, as nationalists have sometimes done, that the resultant Stormont regime represented merely 'sixty years of Stormont misrule'. That regime had substantial achievements to its credit in the economic and infrastructural, educational, social welfare and healthcare fields. Nevertheless, it had fundamental flaws, which revealed themselves from the very beginning of the history of the state.

The flaws might have been less ruinous if the section of the Government of Ireland Act of 1920 providing for formal joint institutions for the whole island of Ireland had been implemented. Although at the beginning there were to be two parliaments and two governments in Ireland, the Act contemplated and afforded every facility for union between North and South, and empowered the two parliaments by mutual agreement and joint action to terminate partition and to set up one parliament and one government for the whole of Ireland. With a view to the eventual establishment of a single parliament, and to bringing about harmonious action between the two parliaments and governments, there was created a bond of union by means of a Council of Ireland, which was to consist of twenty representatives elected by each parliament, and a president nominated by the Lord Lieutenant. It was to fall to the members of that body to initiate proposals for united action on the part of the two parliaments and to bring forward these proposals in the respective parliaments.

The 'Irish dimension', of which there has been so much said by both the British and the Irish governments and by Northern

Ireland nationalists since 1972, is therefore not a new concept. It was formally recognised in the very Act of the British Parliament from which the Northern Ireland state derived and a commitment to give it constitutional embodiment was contained in that same Act.

In the event, Northern Ireland was given a univocally British and unionist constitution, which made no constitutional concessions whatever to the nationalist community and its Irish identity and its aspiration towards an Irish rather than a British union. The division into two states was resorted to because the unionist minority in the island as a whole was too large to be peacefully governed, without its consent, within a united Ireland conceived as a unitary nationalist state. The blunt practical reality in Northern Ireland has been that the nationalist minority within Northern Ireland was and is too large to be peacefully governed without its consent within a Northern Ireland conceived on unitary British and unionist lines.

A Northern Ireland conceived as a unitary British and unionist state has by definition to put a question mark over the legitimacy, the legality and the rights of its non-British and non-unionist people. To be a full and equal citizen of a country is to be fully committed to its constitution, its political institutions, its national symbols. It is a peculiarity of the Northern Ireland constitution in its present form that such an unqualified commitment in effect entails being no longer a nationalist but a unionist. To speak of 'the Northern Ireland people' or 'the Ulster people' when one really means the unionist community, to say, as some spokesmen repeatedly say, such things as 'the Ulster people will never countenance a United Ireland', is to exclude the nationalist people from legitimate citizenship, to define them as non-citizens, indeed as non-people.

The unitary or mono-political model of constitution on which the Northern Ireland state was created had, therefore, a fatal flaw from the beginning. Only a bi-political or bi-polar constitutional model could have worked or would be just to the rights of both communities and would permit reconciliation between them. This flaw was compensated for in some respects in practice by a government that made progress in some areas of administration and made contributions to the common good of both communities. Yet the constitution of itself created an all-pervading sense of alienation in the nationalist community. This sense was aggravated by the experience of inequality of civil and political rights and economic opportunities, and by the experience of discrimination in housing, in employment and in promotion in both the public and the private sector. The Cameron Commission officially acknowledged this, and successive reports of the Fair Employment Agency have supplied abundant documented evidence.

It is all of eighteen years since a British Conservative administration published an analysis of the Northern Ireland situation not altogether different from the analysis I have given above. The discussion paper or Green Paper, as it was called, published in October 1972 under the auspices of the then Secretary of State, William Whitelaw, and entitled *The Future of Northern Ireland: a paper for discussion*, said:

> The special feature of the Northern Ireland situation was that the great divide in political life was not between different viewpoints on such matters as the allocation of resources and the determination of priorities, but between the two whole communities. The 'floating vote' for which rival parties would normally compete was almost non-existent. Thus the relationship between the parties was not fluctuating and uncertain, but virtually fixed from one Election to another. Such a situation was unlikely to foster either sensitivity on the part of the permanent majority, or a sense of responsibility on the part of the permanent minority. [1.14, p. 5]

The same report went on to discuss claims of discrimination practised against the nationalist community by the unionist majority. It concluded:

> What is incontestable is that the continuous and complete control of central government by representatives of the majority alone was virtually bound to give rise to such suspicions. [*Ibid.*, p. 5]

9

The anomalous nature of the constitution and state of Northern Ireland is shown by the persisting difficulty in finding a completely satisfactory and acceptable name for the territory. 'Northern Ireland' has obvious and indeed glaring geographical anomalies. 'Ulster', used as coterminous for the territory, is unacceptable to nationalists because it excludes three Ulster counties. 'The Province' for unionists means a region of Britain, whereas for nationalists it means part of one of the four historic provinces of Ireland. The 'Six Counties' is offensive to unionists. 'Occupied Ireland' is unjust and menacing to unionists because it suggests that Irish unionists are foreign invaders who have no rights in Ireland. The term 'Northern Ireland' is the least unsatisfactory and is becoming generally accepted. Similar difficulty notoriously attaches to the name of Northern Ireland's second city: to call it Derry or to call it Londonderry is not simply to specify a geographical location on the map, it is also implicitly to make a political statement.

The difficulties of nomenclature may seem trivial. But they have importance because they highlight the existence of two communities, with different senses of historical identity and of national self-definition. Some habitual British ways of describing Northern Ireland conceal this fundamental reality. When a government commitment is made to 'maintaining the Union so long as the majority of people in Northern Ireland choose to be British', it should never be forgotten that the spokesman is speaking only of unionists among the Northern Ireland population. He is not speaking of a political majority subject to electoral swings, as in a normal democratic society. Such ways of speaking obscure the real issues. They ignore the fact that a large section of the population do not 'choose to be British'. Political justice requires that every time a guarantee and reassurance of their status and rights is given to unionists, it should be balanced by a parallel guarantee and reassurance to nationalists of their status and rights.

When, as is frequently the case, the terms 'the people of

Northern Ireland' or 'the Ulster people' are used as names for the unionist part of the population, similar obscuration of the real issue is entailed. Such terms in effect define the nationalist population as non-people. They deny the rights of nationalists to that which defines them as nationalists, their attachment to union with the rest of Ireland. 'The people of Northern Ireland' is not solely or homogeneously a unionist people. Commitment to the union of Northern Ireland not with Britain but with the rest of Ireland is the very definition of nationalism, and to aspire and to work peacefully through the political process for that union is the defining characteristic of a nationalist. Nationalism, therefore, by its very definition has to imply some degree of estrangement from a constitution and institutions that are based exclusively and univocally on the principle of the Union; such a constitution and such institutions are by definition unionist. Consequently, what looks like a normal and democratic statement about an ordinary electoral majority amounts in effect to the imposition of a univocally unionist constitution on the nationalist people, who comprise not far short of 40 per cent of the total population. For nationalists, to give full and final and unqualified commitment to the Union would be in effect to abandon nationalism and to become unionists. This is a plain consequence of the meaning and definition of terms. Many civic buildings throughout Northern Ireland have for several years now carried huge placards proclaiming 'ULSTER SAYS NO'. Surely to cover the civic buildings of this land, which belong to all its citizens, with party political slogans that ignore and deny the existence of 40 per cent of those citizens, is not only an injustice and an insult, it is a symptom of political glaucoma, an inability to see and recognise political realities.

It has more recently become common for official statements of British government policy to say that 'Northern Ireland is British because and for as long as a majority of its people are determined to be British.' This formulation is, for nationalists, a significant and welcome step forward from the previously stated position that 'Northern Ireland is as British as Yorkshire.'

11

Nevertheless, this formula also both overstates and understates reality. It identifies territory with people. It thereby constitutionally defines the territory in terms appropriate to its unionist inhabitants, and at the same time defines nationalists out of the territory of Northern Ireland.

What should be said is that the unionist people of Northern Ireland are British and have the right so to be and so to remain for as long as they are determined to be British. This right must be recognised by all and guaranteed. Nationalists within Northern Ireland have precisely equal rights to be and to remain Irish, for as long as they are determined to be Irish. As has been said recently, Northern Ireland 'is not real estate but people', and its people are deeply divided in terms of national identity and politico-national aspiration. This diversity must be reflected in constitutional arrangements and political institutions appropriate to and specific to the unique politico-national duality of its population.

No less objectionable and no less unjust, on the other hand, is the use of the term 'the Irish people', when it is used, as it often is, to refer to the whole population of Ireland. To speak of 'the Irish people's right to self-determination' is in effect to define the unionist population as non-people. It is to deny the rights of unionists to that which defines them as unionists, their attachment to union with Britain. To declaim 'the Irish people's right to self-determination without foreign interference' is tantamount to denying and ignoring the existence of 60 per cent of the population of Northern Ireland. This is equally unjust. It is similarly a disease of the political optic system, an inability to see large and conspicuous political facts. Republicans speak of 'the Irish people' and their right to 'self-determination and national sovereignty' in terms that implicitly exclude the unionist community from membership of the Irish people and effectively define unionists out of existence. To have a rightful place in Ireland or to belong to the Irish people in these republicans' terms, unionists would have to cease to be unionists, for Irish unionists by definition are natives of Ireland who see themselves also as British and who desire to remain politically united with Britain. In other words, republicans identify geographical Ireland with 'the Irish people', and go on to identify 'the Irish people' with the republican/nationalist people. This is quite simply to ignore the basic political reality of the population of Ireland – namely that it includes nearly 1 million people who belong to Ireland but claim also the right to belong to the United Kingdom of Great Britain and Northern Ireland, and who are Irish people but define themselves also as British. The wilder rhetoric of republicanism declares that people who do not wish to belong to the Irish Republic should return to where they properly belong, namely to Britain.

In making comments, politicians have a duty to consider not only the impact of their remarks on their supporters but also the impact their words have on the other community. How are anti-violence nationalists to feel when they are implicitly identified as a cause of 'Ulster's agony and instability'? How are unionists to feel when they are identified as part of the 'occupying forces' in their own homeland? How will the hundreds of thousands of law-abiding and peaceloving members and supporters of the Gaelic Athletic Association throughout Northern Ireland and in Ireland as a whole feel when their great organisation is branded, as it has been, as 'sympathising with terrorism'?

In present circumstances in Northern Ireland our politicians can surely be more careful in their use of language. If politicians cannot bring themselves to use language that promotes trust and respect between the two traditions, surely they could at least refrain from using language that gives offence and insult to one or other of the two traditions whose hope and desire are to share this land in peace and reciprocal respect.

Neither a preclusively unionist status for Northern Ireland nor an exclusively nationalist prescription for Northern Ireland will satisfy the requirements of justice or correspond with plain political realities. Neither will have the remotest chance of securing that minimum consensus that is a precondition for stability and normality in society and that is a prerequisite for the long and hard struggle for economic survival which faces both communities.

13

For more than sixty years, both communities have talked about the marvellous future of justice, equality and partnership we could have had in our country if only 'the others' had not done this or had done that, and about the marvellous future we could now have if 'the others' would only cease doing this or demanding the other. Unionists are repeatedly proclaiming what rights and benefits nationalists would enjoy if only they would give up the aspiration to a united Ireland and accept the forever unalterable and infrangible integrity of Northern Ireland as an integral part of the United Kingdom. Nationalists are no less eloquent in proclaiming how generous nationalist Ireland would be to unionists if only they would 'throw in their lot', or 'get around the table', with their fellow Irishmen and work out the future of our country 'without foreign interference'.

In reality, such speeches are camouflaged statements: by unionists that there can be reconciliation and peace, stability and prosperity in Northern Ireland only when nationalists cease to be nationalists – or else clear out of Northern Ireland; and by nationalists that there can be justice and peace, equality and prosperity in Ireland only when unionists cease to be unionists – or else clear out of Ireland. Both these positions simply run away from the reality that is Northern Ireland. Northern Ireland is a society composed of two communities that have radically conflicting conceptions of the national identity and future of the territory of the state. Both conceptions are equally legitimate political options, and have equal right to be pursued and propagated by peaceful democratic means. Further, the reality of Northern Ireland is that these two communities must find ways of coexisting in peace and equality with one another, without either community demanding of the other that it abnegate its sense of nationhood or renege its political convictions.

## THE CHRISTIAN CHALLENGE

Words of peace and reconciliation are words of life. Words of bitterness and violence are words of death. They conceal a death wish, or they contain an implicit and symbolic murder wish. Those who refuse to dialogue with others, who will not accept the right of others to be different, who will trust or will share with only those 'of our own kind', are secretly wishing that the others were not there, were not alive; they are implicitly willing their death. It is not just by an accident of speech that people say, 'I will cut them dead.' Something like a secret complicity with murder could lurk behind such phrases as, 'Why don't they all go back where they belong?'; 'You can never trust any of them'; 'We must finish this thing now, once and for all.' These phrases can be ways of wishing death to thousands. This is why Christ said that the Commandment 'Thou shalt not kill' forbids us to hate; for hate is a wish that the hated one did not exist. It is a way of wishing him dead. Hate is a symbolic form of murder.

But the last word for Christianity is not death but life, not hate but love. Love was crucified, but it is risen and lives for ever in the One who says, 'I was dead but I am alive and I am to live for ever and ever and I hold keys of death and of the under world' (Apocalypse 1: 17). Because of him we cannot ever despair of peace with justice, reconciliation, forgiveness and love in Ireland. To despair of that would be to despair of God, who 'in Christ is reconciling the world to Himself'. We are Christians because we have believed in love. As St John says, 'We have known and put our faith in God's love towards ourselves' (1 John 4: 16).

To believe in God's love towards ourselves is to believe also in God's love towards others, even when they are different from ourselves. It is to believe in the rights of others to be different from ourselves. The wish to extinguish differences is secretly a wish to eliminate those who dare to differ. Reconciliation across accepted differences is a direct consequence of believing in 'God's love towards ourselves'.

The problems of Northern Ireland are political and social ones, for the solution of which the skill and dedication of political and community leaders are urgently needed. In one sense it is the truth and indeed the whole truth to say that Christian love is the only answer. But love is not a substitute for justice. Love includes justice. Love needs laws, institutions, structures, embodying justice, penalising injustice. When situations and structures exist that militate against justice and impede human dignity and fulfilment, Christian love requires reforms. Reforms in turn demand political action. The Christian call to love our fellow men and women includes the command to remove the conditions that make love unlikely and to build the sort of community structures in which love can grow. Love therefore must be given constitutional and political expression and legal formulation and social embodiment.

The present hour urgently requires politicians to deploy their utmost energies and skills in finding solutions to our critical community problems in Northern Ireland. The contribution of our present-day politicians could be a nobler act of patriotism than any that marks the pages of past history in Ireland. Their positive and peaceful and constructive leadership can be a real witness to Christian faith. Our fervent and continuous prayers will be with the political leaders on all sides, in both parts of Ireland and in Britain, that they may be worthy of the challenge and peril of this hour and that God may make them deserving of His Son's beatitude:

Blessed are the peace-makers;
they shall be called sons of God.
[Matthew 5: 9]

# 2
## THE POLITICAL COST OF PEACE

*To all who bear political responsibility for the affairs of Ire-land, I want to speak with the same urgency and intensity with which I have spoken to the men of violence. Do not cause or condone or tolerate conditions which give excuse or pretext to men of violence. Those who resort to violence always claim that only violence brings about change. They claim that political action cannot achieve justice. You politicians must prove them to be wrong. You must show that there is a peaceful, political way to justice. You must show that peace achieves the work of justice, and violence does not.*

*I urge you who are called to the noble vocation of politics to have the courage to face up to your responsibility, to be leaders in the cause of peace, reconciliation and justice. If politicians do not decide and act for just change, then the field is left open to the men of violence. Violence thrives best when there is a political vacuum and a refusal of political movement.*
[Pope John Paul II, Address at Drogheda, 29 September 1979; in *The Pope in Ireland*, p. 24]

BRITAIN'S RESPONSIBILITY

Nearly every family in Northern Ireland has been affected in one way or another by the twenty-one years of violence: through the death of a friend or relative, the maiming of a loved one, the imprisonment of a parent, a brother or a relative, the bomb destruction of a family business, sectarian intimidation driving people from their home and community. The death toll is now some 2,800 persons. In terms of world catastrophe, this number might seem small. In the small territory of Northern Ireland, the concentration of tragedy has not many parallels. In comparative terms, the number killed is roughly equivalent to the killing by acts of violence of about 94,000 people in Britain. In addition to those killed, there have been more than 21,574 civilians injured or maimed, 9,154 of these as a result of explosions and 1,544 as a result of kneecappings. Many thousands

19

more are suffering from psychological stress related directly to the civil violence.

This litany of tragedies does not include the recurring scenes of street rioting, often involving home-made but potentially lethal petrol bombs or other maiming missiles. Nor does it include the harassment suffered as a result of the varieties of intimidation, protection money, racketeering, inflicted both on the Catholic community by the IRA and on the Protestant community by the loyalist equivalents of the IRA, such as the Ulster Defence Association (UDA), the Ulster Volunteer Force (UVF), the Ulster Freedom Fighters (UFF), etcetera, practices that blur any distinction between politically motivated violence and common crime or mafia-type gang rule. Nor do the statistics include the operations conducted by the security forces, inflicting on peaceful citizens vexation, disturbance of daily and nightly life, and often harassment, and a disturbing number of deaths or grave injuries inflicted through the use of plastic bullets.

All this is happening just one hour's flying time away from London. It is happening in what is officially a region of the United Kingdom and is in theory supposed to be a region as British as Yorkshire. It is happening in a territory where the sole and entire governmental, administrative and security authority and responsibility rests with Westminster. I ask people, particularly in Britain, never to allow the sheer repetitiousness of acts of violence to lessen their sensitivity to the suffering it causes. I ask them not to let anyone wash his or her hands of the problem by blaming it on some peculiar perversity or irrationality of the Irish; and not to feel morally superior towards the Irish as though our conflict were some sort of sixteenth-century religious war incongruously and atavistically dragged on into the late twentieth century. I ask people in Britain to realise that, as I have already emphasised, our problem is a highly complex amalgam of political, constitutional, cultural and historical, as well as religious, differences. I shall attempt to show that it emphatically is not a problem that we ourselves have created or are ourselves culpably perpetuating. I shall try to show that it is not a problem that we can ourselves alone resolve, and that it just will not do to say that the Northern Ireland communities should 'get together and agree between themselves'. I argue, in fact, that the constitutional framework and the institutional arrangements into which we are locked are hampering and hindering movement towards a resolution of our conflict.

Since 1972, with the exception of the brief local power-sharing Executive that governed during a five-month period in 1974, Northern Ireland has been under a regime of direct rule from Westminster. Direct rule was introduced by the British government purely as an interim measure. It was intended to provide a caretaker administration pending the establishment of permanent and equitable structures of government for Northern Ireland. In the discussion paper *The Future of Northern Ireland* of 1972, we read the following about the introduction of direct rule:

> The period of one year for which, unless extended, the Northern Ireland (Temporary Provisions) Act 1972, remains in force, comes to an end on 30 March 1973. While it is possible to extend its application for a further limited period until more permanent arrangements are made, there are strong grounds for keeping such a period to a minimum. The temporary arrangements for the discharge of both law-making and executive responsibilities are not suitable for long-term use. In particular, it would be unsatisfactory to continue indefinitely making important legislative provision for Northern Ireland by way of Orders in Council. Moreover, continuing uncertainty about the future is unsettling to the public service, and can feed the fears and suspicions of a wider public. [p. 36]

The 'temporary arrangements' that were admitted to be unsatisfactory nineteen years ago are still in force, and there is too little evidence of sustained determination and effort by the British government to bring them to an end; nor indeed is there enough evidence of really serious and concentrated thinking at top government level about the form that permanent arrangements must take if they are to be satisfactory and acceptable to both the Northern Ireland communities. It has become clear that Northern Ireland is not anywhere remotely near the centre of preoccupations for the Westminster government. I say with deep seriousness that the situation in Northern Ireland is one of the gravest problems facing the governments of our two islands, and that our best political brains and resources should be devoted to it. Neglect of the Northern Ireland problem would be at the peril of security and even of stability in both our islands. The British and the Irish leader who displays the statesmanship, the determination and the courage to resolve the Northern Ireland problem will truly have earned his or her enduring place in British and in Irish history.

Meanwhile, it would be churlish to deny that direct rule has brought some benefits to Northern Ireland and has remedied some of the unacceptable and discriminatory practices of the former regime. Many of our Secretaries of State worked very hard at reading themselves into the complex political problems of the region and seriously tried to come to grips with them. Longstanding grievances, such as religious discrimination in employment, have been seriously tackled. Many of the successive ministers of state have shown real dedication and genuine social concern, handling their respective portfolios with efficiency and impartiality and trying, in difficult economic circumstances, to pay particular attention to the needs of the most deprived areas.

Nevertheless, the system of direct rule is in itself a radically unsatisfactory system. A mood of complacency has developed in respect of it, and I am convinced that this complacency carries many dangers. The most obvious damaging consequence is that regional politics become paralysed and regional political parties become marginalised. There is little incentive for people of talent and commitment to enter politics or to remain in political life. Mere discussion, without any power of decision or of execution, becomes trivialised. It quickly comes to be seen as mere tokenism and is readily dismissed as irrelevant. Unionism has become dangerously fragmented and is under a constant pull to the right from extremist groupings. This situation can bring no joy even to non-unionists. It bodes ill for the future of this society.

Nationalist political parties also become marginalised. Constitutional nationalism is endangered as a peaceful and constitutional political movement. It should not be forgotten that mainstream nationalism in Northern Ireland in the past twenty years has evolved very significantly. It repudiates violence. It has abandoned abstentionism. It gives *de facto* recognition to the institutions of the Northern Ireland state and relies exclusively on peaceful and constitutional means of advancing nationalist aspirations. This is a relatively new phenomenon in politics in Northern Ireland. It is a phenomenon that offered and continues to offer unprecedented opportunities for peaceful change and peaceful political movement in the direction of an inter-community political consensus, without which no political stability can be restored in Northern Ireland. It is a great tragedy of the past two decades that the opportunities offered by the new evolution of nationalism were not seized. It will be a still greater tragedy if this evolution is put at risk by continuing political intransigence and deadlock.

Dissatisfaction with direct rule is felt both by the unionist and the nationalist communities. Here is what the Ulster Unionist Party has to say about it, in their document *The Way Forward*, presented in 1984:

> The present system of direct rule is the subject of justifiable criticism in that it is often inaccessible to local opinion, insensitive to local views, and politically unaccountable to the Northern Ireland electorate. The most basic services such as health, education, housing, and the environment, which matter so much to every citizen, are the subject of no real democratic control. The essential services, as well as others, are administered by the civil servants of the relevant departments of the Northern Ireland Office who are answerable only to the Secretary of State for Northern Ireland and his team of junior ministers. Delay in decision making and consequent frustration are the inevitable result when bureaucrats are not accountable to any electorate . . .
>
> In only one part of the United Kingdom, namely, Northern Ireland, are major services subject to no real democratic control. In Northern Ireland alone do employees and professional staff who would normally take their instructions directly from

elected representatives, take orders from the civil servants of the Government Departments at Stormont. There are in Northern Ireland, no indigenous representatives who decide and direct policy on major services, and who themselves are answerable to their electorates for their stewardship. The Stormont civil servants are answerable to no-one but the Secretary of State for Northern Ireland and his team of ministers, all of whom are on short term commissions.

The *Report of the New Ireland Forum* (1984) acknowledged this unionist alienation saying:

> There is fear, insecurity, confusion and uncertainty about the future in the unionist section of the community. Northern Ireland today is characterised by the fact that neither section of the community is happy with the status quo or has confidence in or a sense of direction about the future. It is essential that any proposals for political progress should remove nationalist alienation and assure the identity and security of both unionists and nationalists. [Section 2.6]

New and hard thinking in Westminster is required. New institutions are needed, and cannot be indefinitely postponed: institutions that do not merely give a forum for repeating hackneyed political slogans but that provide some mechanism for uncoupling deadlocked positions. It would be paradoxical if Britain's rightly celebrated genius for political sagacity were to fail in respect of a territory on her own doorstep, which 'the Mother of Parliaments' directly rules. Mutual accusations between Church and government are not to be lightly indulged in. Yet I believe that neither the British nor the Irish governments have yet worked out a sufficiently fundamental analysis of the Northern problem and translated that analysis into a coherent and consistent policy.

The Westminster government, it must be firmly stated, has, as of now, direct and supreme responsibility for governing Northern Ireland. It consequently has primary responsibility for working with all the interests involved towards a solution of its problems. This solution must be worked out in dialogue with both communities. It must be acceptable to both

24

communities. But the primary responsibility rests with West-minster. There must be no hand-washing and no complacency. There is no such thing as 'an acceptable level of violence' in any corner of these islands. The stability, the welfare, the inter-national repute of both our countries is at stake. The Northern conflict does not reflect some peculiarly Irish perversity. If – as I pray will not happen – an area of Britain were to be afflicted with similar violence stemming from similar causes, I believe its inhabitants might cope less successfully and less cheerfully with them than the Northern Ireland community has coped.

It should therefore be with a fitting humility, as well as with a non-judgemental concern, that Westminster faces its task of finding a solution that will provide Northern Ireland with a credible and acceptable settlement, accepted by both commu-nities as safeguarding the just rights of each. I believe there are few more grave or urgent problems facing the British govern-ment today.

It will not do to pass the blame to Northern Ireland parties or people. Intransigent political attitudes notoriously do exist and are deplorable and disastrous. But they are not simply the fruit of ill will. They are also in part caused by inappropriate and inequitable political institutions. Political movement and the possibility of political change are of the essence of democratic politics, and political institutions that inhibit movement and change are inimical to the democratic process.

All politicians in Britain have responsibilities in respect of Ireland. After major atrocities the Westminster Parliament takes a sudden and fevered interest in Irish affairs. With honourable exceptions, its interest is too often confined to the latest atroc-ity perpetrated in Britain itself and the reaction is often confined to calls for tougher security measures. There is little continuing concern about Ireland's problems and too little recognition of Britain's responsibility in the original creation of these problems and in their perpetuation. In Britain, there is too little under-standing in depth of Irish affairs and too little awareness of Irish sensitivities and rights. It is an urgent need that Anglo-Irish relations be conducted on a firm basis of reciprocity and mutual trust. It is an urgent necessity that the British government have a sustained and realistic policy for tackling the social, economic, industrial and environmental neglect that west and north Belfast and other deprived areas of Northern Ireland have for so long suffered, and should put in place a systematic and integrated programme of overall rehabilitation, making available all the expertise and resources that a critical situation demands. We must show that there is a peaceful and constitutional way to justice, and that it works.

Another contribution that British politicians and the British government could make to an atmosphere of reconciliation in Ireland would be to use their good offices to discourage the anti-Irish hysteria that on occasions marks the popular press in Britain. There is no longer an anti-British bias in Irish media comparable to the anti-Irish bias one sometimes finds in elements of the British media. There is much more accurate information and much better-informed comment about British affairs in Irish media than vice versa. The misinformation and misconceptions in Britain about Irish political parties and their leaders – sometimes, unfortunately, aided by Irish commentators – are abysmal and, in present circumstances, dangerous. Britain has everything to gain from cultivating genuine friendship with Ireland and from reciprocating and positively promoting the genuine goodwill towards Britain that characterises Ireland now. Britain's honour as well as Britain's interest require good relationships with Ireland at this time.

As I have argued above, the British government has defined Northern Ireland's problem in terms of its two identities. The White Paper *Northern Ireland – A Framework for Devolution*, presented to Parliament by the then Secretary of State for Northern Ireland, Jim Prior, in April 1982, said:

> The majority of the population in Northern Ireland think of themselves as British. They regard themselves as part of the social and cultural fabric of the United Kingdom and their loyalty lies to the Crown. They favour continuance of the union with rest of the United Kingdom . . . There is also a substantial minority within Northern Ireland who think of themselves as

Irish, whether in terms of their identity, their social and cultural traditions, or their political aspirations. Many of them support political parties which would like to see a united Ireland in some form.

This difference in identity and aspiration lies at the heart of the 'problem' of Northern Ireland; it cannot be ignored or wished away. [Sections 3.14–3.15, 3.17]

A territory like Northern Ireland, with two diverse communities and lacking constitutional consensus, must be given a constitution and political institutions reflecting its diversity. A unitary unionist constitutional model for Northern Ireland has not worked and will not work. It is unjust. It ignores the existence and denies the political rights of nationalists. Similarly, a unitary nationalist constitutional model for a united Ireland would not work and would be unjust. It would ignore the existence and deny the political rights of unionists.

The appeal for a change of heart from which peace can be born must, therefore, be addressed firstly to the British government. It was Britain who devised and imposed the faulty constitution from which our present problems ultimately stem. It is Britain that today has the major responsibility for correcting its defects. Constitutional arrangements appropriate to a bi-polar population must be worked out as a basis for a just and permanent settlement in Ireland. This just settlement of the Irish problem must be seen as one of Britain's major national interests, and even as one of her prime responsibilities to the European and international community.

The logic of what I have been saying points inescapably in the first instance to that minimum of constitutional adjustment that will make it possible for nationalists to identify with the constitution and the institutions of Northern Ireland without having to become unionists in order to do so. It implies the giving of full constitutional legitimacy to the nationalist identity. In the words of the *Report of the New Ireland Forum*:

> The validity of both the nationalist and unionist identities in Ireland and the democratic right of every citizen on this land must be accepted; both of these identities must have equally

27

satisfactory, secure and durable, political, administrative and symbolic expression and protection. [Section 5.2(4), p. 27]

The logic of the two identities analysis is that political institutions must be provided that permit an allocation of proportionate political power to each of the identities, for politics is about power, power controlled by accountability, but yet real power of decision and of execution. Politics without power is mere roleplaying. Failure to provide the political institutions that enable power to be exercised proportionately and responsibly by the two admitted identities comprising the population of Northern Ireland is a political failure; responsibility for this political failure is shared by the British government, which alone and directly now governs the area, and by those Irish politicians who refuse dialogue or who pose impossible and unrealistic preconditions for dialogue.

'INTERNAL NORTHERN IRELAND SOLUTION'

The logic of my remarks might be held to point to what has been called an 'internal Northern Ireland solution', even if one that would give recognition and expression to the two political and national identities or traditions in Northern Ireland. I turn now to an examination of the semantics and the logic of the 'internal Northern Ireland solution'.

As I have already emphasised, Northern Ireland is composed of two communities, a unionist one and a nationalist one, with two distinct identities and traditions. To be a unionist is to be committed to the British constitution and to British nationality and citizenship, with all the reality and the symbolism of the British national flag and anthem and emblems, etcetera, which go therewith. This is the British dimension. To be a constitutional nationalist is to be committed to Irish nationality and citizenship, and to aspire, by a peaceful political process and through consensus, towards the eventual reunification of Ireland; and to be consequently entitled to the constitutional recognition and the institutional and symbolic expression of that Irish identity, including the Irish national flag and anthem and emblems, etcetera, which go therewith. This is the Irish dimension.

It is to be understood that neither identity and neither set of symbols can be allowed to be asserted or displayed in ways that are provocative to the other community.

By the typical unionist, the concept of an Irish dimension is regarded as 'interference by a foreign power in the internal affairs of the United Kingdom'. By many nationalists, the concept of a British dimension is regarded as 'a foreign intervention in the internal affairs of Ireland'. What has to be affirmed unequivocally and with emphasis is that *both* the Irish and the British dimensions are *internal* to Northern Ireland. Both the Irish dimension and the British dimension are precisely the basic ingredients of the so-called 'internal Northern Ireland solution'. The British dimension is not the presence of an alien and foreign British administration and the British Army: it is embodied in the lawful political convictions and basic political rights of nearly 1 million inhabitants of Northern Ireland. But it is equally true that the Irish dimension is not the interference of a foreign and alien state in the internal affairs of Northern Ireland. The Irish dimension is embodied in the equally lawful convictions and equally basic political rights of nearly 600,000 inhabitants of Northern Ireland.

In this sense, an 'internal Northern Ireland solution' has to be also a British/Irish solution. In other words, an 'internal' solution has to be concomitantly external to the territory of Northern Ireland, and this in a two-directional sense. The very same principles of political justice that legitimise a British governmental presence in the affairs of Northern Ireland equally legitimise an Irish governmental presence in the affairs of Northern Ireland. This is because the internal political composition of the Northern Ireland problem itself points outside Northern Ireland, and points in two different directions: one towards London and the British Parliament and government, the other towards Dublin and the Irish Parliament and government. Unless these facts are kept in mind, the concept of an 'internal Northern Ireland solution' misrepresents

29

the internal realities of Northern Ireland and obscures the real issues.

The fact is that Northern Ireland has never been given constitutional arrangements or political institutions appropriate to the internal composition of its nationally and politically polarised population. This fact must now be faced squarely. It is a matter of urgency to undertake now with courage and determination the process that will at last provide those constitutional arrangements and establish those institutions.

The notion of repartition has been mooted. This formula would merely make a bad situation worse. Repartition of Northern Ireland, with the effect of creating a smaller territory within which the unionist majority would be overwhelming, would still leave nearly a quarter of a million nationalists within that unionist state, and would leave them more hopelessly condemned than ever to perpetual minority status and therefore to irremediable alienation.

## A CHANGE OF HEART BY UNIONISTS

I am very conscious that I have no right to speak to unionists, much less to speak for them. Nevertheless, since Protestants and Catholics share the same commitment to Christ's kingdom of righteousness, love and peace, and since the welfare of one community is inextricably bound up with the welfare of the other, I wish to be allowed to put some reflections to unionists for their Christian consideration.

Republican paramilitaries seek support for violence and receive some support for violence on the basis of a claim that there is no other way of breaking the political impasse created by the intransigence of unionist politicians. They argue that politics has offered no solution and can offer no solution; that no one has offered or has any apparent intention of offering a political alternative to violence. It is vital, in all our interests, that this claim be deprived of all credibility.

It is essential that the present political immobilism in Northern Ireland be ended. It is imperative that political leaders demonstrate their readiness to talk with one another and to work with one another in devising political alternatives to inter-community strife. If unionists refuse and continue to repeat out-of-date 'no surrender' slogans, violence will go on indefinitely. Given constitutional forms and institutions with which both communities could identify, unionists and nationalists could join energies, talents and skills to rebuild our shattered economy and make this region a place where we could all live with pride and our young people have reasons for hope, leaving the long-term political and constitutional future of Northern Ireland and of the island as a whole to peaceful, political evolution.

This will not happen unless politicians face up to the challenge of change. If they do, the remaining vestiges of sympathy and support would quickly be removed from the paramilitaries, and reconstruction for both communities could begin. Politics is about change. It is about peaceful change in the interests of justice through consensus.

The dilemma of unionism is that it has claimed over a whole territory rights that properly belong only to the unionist community as one of the political communities within that territory. Territoriality and national allegiance normally coincide; where they do not, conflicts are virtually inevitable. These conflicts can be avoided only when constitutional arrangements and political institutions are devised that reflect the politically bi-polar nature of the community and give minority communities their full political and civil rights. Unionism, however, supported by the British government, seeks to impose on a whole territory a unionist constitution that gives no recognition to nearly two-fifths of its population and that therefore deprives nearly 600,000 people of constitutional legitimacy. There are not many examples in the Western world today of regimes whose constitution reflects the party policy of only one political community among the political communities within the population of the territory.

One can sympathise with the dilemma of unionism. But it is a consequence of history, with which nationalists as well as unionists have to come to terms. Neither unionists nor

31

nationalists can be constitutionally defined out of existence. Neither community can be deprived of its rights.

I should like to appeal to fair-minded unionists. I ask them to recognise how deeply hurtful and how unjust it is to a community of nearly 600,000 people to be denied full and equal citizenship in their own country. It is surely inconsistent to expect nationalists to accept in Northern Ireland a status that unionists vehemently refuse for themselves in a united Ireland. The just claims and peaceful aspirations of democratic nationalists are no threat to unionists. They are a threat only to an inequality of rights, which makes society unstable for unionism itself. The unionist and loyalist parties and their spokespersons rarely speak of nationalists except as enemies. They almost never speak of them as fellow citizens with whom they are willing and ready to share the land in equity and in partnership. The Ulster Unionist Party is ostensibly the more moderate of the two main unionist/loyalist parties. Yet in its documents and in the speeches of its politicians this party invariably speaks of nationalists as enemies of the state, people with whom the sharing of power and responsibility would be unthinkable. In the habitual language of the party, any 'concession' made to nationalists would endanger the institutions of the state.

Unionists have felt quite justified in refusing or restricting the rights of nationalists. Frank Millar, formerly secretary of the Ulster Unionist Party, has written:

> Unionists in 1968 were generally quite straightforward in their attitude to the civil rights movement. Simply put, they saw it as a threat to 'the constitution' – the pretext for a campaign to destabilise the State. While [others] will record the disappointment of some civil rights leaders that a campaign for 'justice' gave way to one of murderous violence, most Unionist activists even today will dismiss such protestations as naive or disingenuous.

James Molyneaux, in his address as party leader to the 1984 annual Ulster Unionist Party Conference, declared: 'No framework can contain those who want to remain in the United Kingdom and those whose short, medium and long term determination it is to end the United Kingdom status.' Surely the party leader can scarcely have meant to say this, for the statement as it stands means that there is no place in Northern Ireland for constitutional nationalists.

At the party's 1988 conference the same speaker dismissed the demands of constitutional nationalist politicians as 'the whinges of never-satisfied republicans'. He seemed to be referring to all nationalists when he spoke of 'that element which for a century has plotted Ulster's downfall'. One unionist writer wrote about what he called the 'terrorist community'; he was referring to west Belfast. He seemed oblivious to the outrageous slur he was casting upon tens of thousands of people in west Belfast who have suffered from terrorism much more than he has and detest it as strongly as he does.

Unionists traditionally felt and presumably still feel that if nationalists live within the territory of the United Kingdom and share what unionists believe to be its privileges, then they ought to give unequivocal recognition to its constitution, give allegiance to the Crown, and declare their unqualified acceptance of the legitimacy and permanence of the institutions of the Northern Ireland state. The official unionist position has not significantly changed, and the parallel between its attitude to nationalists' rights and the Sinn Féin attitude to unionists' rights seems uncannily close. Sinn Féin's ultimate solution for the Irish problem, we are told, would be 'a settlement based on Northern Protestants throwing in their lot with the rest of the Irish people . . . and in the process tapping the democratic potential of a Protestant tradition freed from its association with Unionism'. I suggest that an accurate translation of the unionist position could run as follows: Nationalists are offered a settlement based on Northern Ireland nationalists throwing in their lot with the rest of the Ulster people . . . and in the process tapping the democratic potential of a Catholic tradition freed from its association with nationalism.

James Molyneaux has spoken of the possibility and the desirability of unionist dialogue with Roman Catholics, as distinct from dialogue with nationalists. I believe that it is fair to suggest that what is being said is that Catholics will have every right guaranteed to them within Northern Ireland when and if they become unionists. Nationalists will have full equality of rights with other Ulster men and women when and if they become unionists. Unless and until they do so, they remain, in unionist thinking, a threat to the constitution, a disloyal element committed to the destabilising of the state.

Is it not time for unionist politicians to show some generosity of spirit, some expression of goodwill, towards those Irish nationalist Northern Ireland people to whom this land belongs as much as it belongs to unionist/British Northern Ireland people? After all, constitutional nationalists are by definition people who are willing and anxious to work peacefully and under the law and through the political process within the institutions of Northern Ireland, willing and anxious to co-operate with unionists for the common good and prosperity of both communities, while abjuring all violence and relying exclusively on political dialogue and persuasion to pursue and promote their nationalist objectives. Why cannot unionists accept their good faith? Nationalists in Northern Ireland did not always follow this path. Their present and now well-established policy surely offers a new opportunity to unionists. Why cannot unionists seize this opportunity? Surely it is high time that unionists should publicly and officially express their recognition of constitutional Irish nationalism and of its aspirations to a united Ireland as a fully legitimate constituent part of the political reality that is Northern Ireland.

I wish that unionist spokespersons would realise how offensive it is to peaceloving and law-abiding nationalists to be referred to as disloyal, as enemies of the state, as differing only in methods from the IRA. The difference between constitutional nationalists and the IRA and their political advocates is a fundamental political, moral and philosophical difference, it is a difference in kind and not just in method. It is insulting to constitutional nationalists to suggest otherwise. It is time that unionist leaders publicly recognised this and gave a lead to their followers in calling for recognition of it.

Thinking unionists will surely see that they cannot hope to defy the decisions or overturn the solemn international commitments of the British government, which they recognise as their own government. The unionist community cannot go it alone in terms of the British government. Neither can it go it alone without the consent and co-operation of the nationalist community. Unionists and nationalists both should readily welcome new opportunities of working towards a new and peaceful and better future for themselves, as well as for the other community. Unionists must, even in their own interests, give a responsible, even if cautious and critical, reception and a fair chance to institutions that, to adapt words from the Ulster Unionist Party's own document *The Way Forward*, can enable nationalists to feel that Northern Ireland belongs to them as well as to the unionists. Simply from the point of view of unionists' own self-interest, such a change of attitude on their part would go far to undermine the credibility of paramilitary republicanism. Ulster Unionist Party MP Ken Maginnis recently remarked, 'I would be of use to the IRA if I was divisive within the community – but I try not to be, and hence I am a hindrance to them' (*Independent*, 10 September 1990).

UNCERTAINTY ABOUT THE CONSTITUTIONAL POSITION?

It is often claimed on the unionist side that the greatest weakness in Northern Ireland's present situation is the uncertainty and ambiguity surrounding its long-term constitutional position. It is argued that the greatest need is for an unambiguous declaration that Northern Ireland will perpetually and irrevocably remain part of the United Kingdom. Shortly before Ian Gow was brutally murdered by the IRA in 1990, he wrote an introduction to a new pamphlet by the Friends of the Union Group. In it he said, 'The Friends of the Union believe that the most important single factor in prolonging the tragedy in Northern Ireland is continuing uncertainty about Ulster's constitutional position.' About this it has to be said that uncertainty about the constitutional position and long-term future of Northern

Ireland comes from within the politico-demographic structure of Northern Ireland itself. It does not come from any interference from outside Northern Ireland. It does not come from any territorial claim in the Constitution of the Republic of Ireland. The nature of the uncertainty is such that it cannot be removed by any Act of Parliament or government declaration or decree on the part of the Parliament and government of Great Britain. It cannot be removed by any constitutional amendment or other act on the part of the Parliament and government and people of the Republic of Ireland.

In the short term, Northern Ireland's constitutional position must in justice recognise the internal political and national diversity that makes Northern Ireland unlike any region in Britain, makes it, as Kevin Boyle and Tom Hadden have described it: 'a place apart from the mainstream of politics in both Ireland and Britain, a frontier zone where people of two states intermingle, and which for that reason needs special treatment'. In the long term, the constitutional position of Northern Ireland will be determined by the evolution of the political process between its two communities and by democratic dialogue between its two traditions. No British government declaration or action can secure, much less impose, an internal consensus within Northern Ireland for a future within the United Kingdom and thereby guarantee an irreversible British constitutional position for the indefinite future. No Irish government declaration or act can secure or impose, even if it wanted to, internal consensus within Northern Ireland for a future within an Irish Ireland and thereby guarantee a united Ireland constitutional position in the indefinite future. Even when both the British dimension and the Irish dimension, with all their constitutional and political implications, have been fully and effectively recognised, the future of Northern Ireland can be determined only by the communities living within Northern Ireland.

A CHANGE OF HEART BY NATIONALISTS

As a Christian pastor, I have no right to take up political positions or to speak on behalf of any political grouping. To

36

identify the Christian faith with any political party is a prostitution of the Gospel. I am bound, however, by my office to endeavour to apply the Gospel message to today's political realities and to indicate the moral parameters within which the Gospel values of peace and justice must be pursued. In the words of Pope John Paul II (Message for World Day of Peace, 1 January 1985), I am bound to try to help Catholics 'to become more aware of situations that are out of harmony with the Gospel, in order to purify and rectify them'. I must therefore say to nationalists that this is a time for making new departures in co-operation, for taking new and positive initiatives to demonstrate still more strongly and clearly their unambiguous repudiation of all violence, their renunciation of any desire to dominate or to coerce, and their readiness to share responsibility and work in constructive partnership with unionists for the welfare of the whole community.

Nationalists speak of 'fifty years of Stormont misrule'. This language has a basis in nationalists' experience because the name Stormont is associated for them with exclusion, rejection, denial of civic and political legitimacy and equality, refusal of entry into many areas of employment, discrimination in many sectors of social and economic life. Yet nationalists must also in fairness acknowledge that the Stormont regime had notable successes and achievements to its credit. Many of those involved at the level of administration and the public service strove to redress the basic bias that frequently was manifested at political level. At the level of administration and of the civil service, Catholics often experienced understanding and co-operation, for example in the development of the Catholic school system and in the administration of social services. Under Stormont, there was notable progress in educational planning, in infrastructural development, in health care and in social welfare provision. Since the establishment of the Northern Ireland Housing Executive there has been fairness in housing allocation and outstanding progress in housing provision. The Republic of Ireland could learn much, in many of these areas, from Northern Ireland.

Ample evidence was given that there exists in Northern Ireland real talent for political administration – evidence enough to point up the misfortune of the atrophying of that talent by the indefinite prolongation of direct rule. It is easy to understand that Stormont came to be a source of pride to unionists. It was a symbol of their security and an apparent guarantee of the permanence of their domination. The dissolution of Stormont has caused a great and unprecedented insecurity and uncertainty among unionists. It has led to distrust of Britain, fear of the Irish Republic, suspicion of Roman Catholics and nationalists, a sense of being alone and threatened.

All this should bring no joy and no triumphalism to Catholics and nationalists. We are all fellow countrymen, fellow Irishmen. Ireland is the home of unionists as well as of nationalists, and no one should feel threatened in his own home. It is the duty of nationalists and constitutional republicans to convince unionists, in word and in behaviour, that they have nothing to fear and that their suspicions are groundless so far as nationalism is concerned. An Ireland that has no room for 1 million Irishmen will not have room for the remaining 3 million either. Such an Ireland might, in Yeats's words, have much hatred; but it will have little room for anyone to live in peace. Above all, as Christians we know that we are brothers and sisters together and that God is Father of us all. We cannot come to Our Father without our brothers and sisters, for we are their keepers; this implies that we are also the defenders of their rights and interests.

Nationalists have already, in fact, formally declared their recognition of the right of unionists to be unionist and therefore British. They did so in the New Ireland Forum, which presented its conclusions in 1984. The New Ireland Forum had its defects and its disappointments, but it did arrive at a consensus statement by all constitutional nationalists within the island of Ireland of the nationalist attitude to unionist rights. That a consensus between all constitutional nationalist parties was achieved was itself a significant event. What was without precedent in the modern history of Irish nationalism was the fact

38

that this nationalist consensus included the recognition by nationalists of the right of unionists to be and to remain unionist
and the explicit recognition that this included their right to be
and to remain British. The Forum declared:

> A redefined relationship between Britain and Ireland would take
> account of the unionist sense of Britishness. In a unitary state,
> persons in Ireland, North and South, who at present hold British
> citizenship would continue to have such citizenship and could
> pass it on to their children without prejudice to the status of
> Irish citizenship which they would automatically acquire. The
> state could develop structures, relationships and associations
> with Britain which could include an Irish–British Council with
> intergovernmental and interparliamentary structures which would
> acknowledge the unique relationship between Ireland and Britain
> and which would provide expression of the long-established
> connections which unionists have with Britain. [*Report of the New
> Ireland Forum*, section 6.6]

The report goes on to say that the solution to both the historical
problem and the current crisis of Northern Ireland and the continuing problem of relations between Ireland and Britain necessarily
requires new structures that will accommodate together two sets
of legitimate rights: 'the right of nationalists to effective political,
symbolic and administrative expression of their identity' and 'the
right of unionists to effective political, symbolic and administrative
expression of their identity, their ethos and their way of life' (*ibid.*,
section 4.15). Unionists may well argue that this or that stance of
Northern Ireland constitutional nationalists, this or the other declaration of Irish politicians, this or that legislation or policy or
practice of the Irish government is inconsistent with this declaration. But they should not ignore the significance of the declaration
itself. I believe that it needs further elucidation by nationalists of
its implications for present political and institutional arrangements
as well as for eventual future political and institutional structures.
I believe further that the Forum declaration provides a basis for
dialogue between nationalists and unionists and that this dialogue
is required specifically of nationalists by the logic of the Forum
process.

Nationalism aspires to a united island of Ireland. There is no way that it can attain this aim other than through persuasion of unionists to consent, and through the elaboration, in dialogue with unionists, of political arrangements and institutions acceptable also to unionists. All except a small fraction of nationalists on this island are agreed that to use physical force to bring about unity is self-contradictory and self-defeating, morally wrong and the source of grievous damage to the whole of Ireland. No chanting of republican slogans will alter these facts. Nationalism can succeed only by persuasion through dialogue and through its readiness to respect and accommodate the British identity and United Kingdom allegiance of unionists under institutions acceptable to both communities. No democratic political party could ask from its political opponents more than this. If nationalism did not believe that this is possible, then it would have ceased to believe in itself or in the democratic process. If unionism did not believe that this was legitimate and acceptable, then it would have ceased to believe in itself or in the democratic process.

Cannot nationalists tell unionists what is the place of unionists in the Irish nationalist perspective now, and not just in the all-Ireland future of nationalist hopes? What is the nationalist view of the unionists' right to be and to remain unionist, to be and to remain British? What is the nationalist view of the institutions of the Northern Ireland state and of nationalist participation in them; what is their view of the courts, the police and security forces, of nationalist participation in the functions and agencies of government at central, regional and local level and in statutory bodies? Considered and reasoned statements of this kind from political parties on each side, statements intended to be seriously discussed among parties on the other side, would be at least a preparation for the talks that must eventually come and would go some way towards substituting constructive dialogue for sterile and dreary diatribe.

DUBLIN'S CONTRIBUTION TO DIALOGUE

The Irish government too has a part to play in the effort at dialogue. The first and the most urgent call from the North to the political parties in the Republic is that they strictly refrain from making Northern Ireland's troubles a party political issue or an element of any electioneering platform. To do so would be a grave disservice to both nationalist and unionist communities in the North and to the hopes of peace.

It is also important that the Irish government and the Republic's political parties see themselves not solely as concerned about the nationalist community and its rights but also as concerned about the unionist community; unionists too are part of the people of Ireland and unionists' rights and their welfare, their sensitivities and their fears must be a matter of concern to anyone who claims to speak for and to serve the Irish people.

VISION FOR A MORE EUROPEAN IRELAND

A new Europe is being formed before our eyes. The iron mould in which the shape of Europe seemed to have been fixed for all foreseeable time has been dramatically, even miraculously, broken. Surely that constitutes both a rebuke and a challenge to us and an inspiration and a source of hope.

Whatever the eventual configuration of this new Europe – and there are many uncertainties and grave risks ahead – France and Germany will certainly play a vital role as continental axis. When one thinks of the hostilities, hates and hurts that divided these two people, the cemeteries across Europe that hold the victims of their blood-lettings in three wars within seventy-five years, and now sees them make common cause in the construction of a new Europe 'without frontiers and without wars', one must take hope for the ending of our conflict too. One great symbol of French resistance to the historic German enemy was Verdun. For half a century Verdun stood as a great emotional monument to French national pride and patriotic sentiment. Yet a few years ago President Mitterrand and Chancellor Kohl were able to stand beside one another at Verdun and shake hands in a common pledge to renounce war and work together for a future of peace.

Relationships between the divided communities in Northern Ireland and between Northern unionists and the rest of Ireland, relationships between the Republic of Ireland and Britain must not remain unaffected while relationships all over Europe are being transformed. Unionists should see the value and importance, in European terms and indeed in historical terms, of improved relations between the Republic of Ireland and Britain. That historic quarrels and misunderstandings between these two island neighbours should be replaced by mutual trust and co-operation could not but be good for all of Ireland and would be in line with what is happening between ancient enemies and between East and West in continental Europe. Indeed it could serve as a model for other areas divided by memories of ancient wrongs. Partisan concerns should not prevent people in Northern Ireland from welcoming and encouraging those improved relationships.

If committed Christians, 'children of light' (Luke 16: 8), whose calling is to walk in the light (1 John 1: 7) and to live in love (1 John 4: 16) fail to work to earn the trust of other committed Christians and to trust them, from where can light and hope come to our troubled land? God loves and accepts us as we are, loves us while we are still sinners (Romans 5: 8), and by loving us changes us. We must love others as they are, accept them as they are, not demand that first they change and then we will love them. Even if we want others to change we must begin by loving and accepting them in their differences.

In the Europe that beckons us as we approach 1992, Northern Ireland and the Republic of Ireland have common interests and shared needs; we have similar difficulties to overcome, similar opportunities to grasp. We have everything to gain from co-operation and partnership. Political differences need not impede this co-operation. Political convictions should not and need not be compromised by it. Let us not draw back from a path that is for our mutual benefit because of fear as to where it might lead. The slogan 'Sinn Féin' means 'ourselves alone'. There are unionist versions of it as well as nationalist versions. There are unionist 'Sinn Féiners' as well as nationalist ones.

Such attitudes must be rethought in the context of Europe. We can still be ourselves while co-operating with others. Indeed 'ourselves alone' must be replaced in both communities by 'ourselves with the others'. Surely that is also the Christian way.

## A CHANGE OF HEART BY PARAMILITARY REPUBLICANS

It cannot be repeated too often that there can be no conceivable political arrangements in Ireland, now or in the future, that fail to accommodate two diverse traditions and to respect the identity and rights of both. There can be no just future for either of the two communities in Northern Ireland until each comes to respect the rights and identity of the other. Violence from either community against the other only prolongs misery for both.

The opportunities for political consensus are seriously threatened by the campaign of violence by paramilitary republicans. This campaign is a blatant contradiction of the attempt by paramilitary republicanism to present itself as a political movement. This attempt is contradicted by the claim of this movement to combine two incompatible elements: the armalite and the ballot box. If the moves by the IRA towards political involvement represented a genuine will to enter into the democratic process they could only be welcomed. But a choice must be made. Republicans must choose either physical force or democratic persuasion. They cannot have both. The armalite and the ballot box cannot be carried together. The democratic process and, indeed, civilisation itself consists in, as the philosopher A. N. Whitehead declared, 'the victory of persuasion over force'. We all have known regimes where the voting booths were ringed with screens of armalites and tanks. These regimes were able to command up to 99 per cent majorities. Which of us will call them democratic? Which of us would wish to live under them? The campaign of violence by paramilitary republicans includes as part of its strategy the assassination of fellow Irishmen simply because they embrace different political convictions and translate these convictions, as is their right, into

43

defence against physical force of the institutions embodying their convictions. The recent murder of Ian Gow is only the latest in a series of murders of politicians whose only crime was to espouse and campaign for political convictions opposed to those of Irish republicans. A republican spokesman, purporting to justify this murder, spoke of the intention to diversify 'targets', military, economic and political. Any group that claims or supports a 'right' to murder political opponents stands self-excluded from the political process.

Just as unionists are fully justified in maintaining their political convictions, they are also justified in believing in the right and the duty under law to defend these political institutions against the threat of overthrow by armed uprising. There are some who choose to do so by service in the security forces or in the police force. There are also people, and not all of them are unionists, who believe that in any civilised society there must be normal policing, and who therefore choose policing as a career of service to the whole Northern Ireland community. The republican paramilitary campaign of assassination of members of the Ulster Defence Regiment (UDR) and Royal Ulster Constabulary (RUC) is equivalent to a campaign of shooting fellow Irishmen simply because they have different political convictions from nationalists. An added enormity of this campaign is that in the actual circumstances of Northern Ireland it is inevitable that unionists and Protestants should regard the assassination of Protestant members of these forces as murders of Protestants because they are Protestants. It is inevitable, particularly in border areas, that the Protestant community should see such assassinations as a sectarian murder campaign and should feel itself threatened by it with expulsion from their homes and lands and businesses.

No group that engages in campaigns of this kind can honestly and credibly claim to be a true political movement. Such campaigns are also a negation of the concept of policing as a necessary protection of law and life and property and of the right of men and women to sleep in peace in their own homes and of the right of children to cross the road to school in safety

– the protection of which rights by the police is a basic requisite in any society. The IRA have killed policemen in the act of discharging these basic services to the whole community. Paramilitary republicanism and its political fronts cannot rightly present themselves as political organisations unless and until they give up the armalite, reject assassination and repudiate physical force as instruments for the advancement of their political aims.

It would be in the general interest that paramilitary republicans should fully enter the political process, but they must accept the consequences of this decision. I would like to appeal to thinking people among the republican paramilitaries. If they believe in republicanism as an ideal capable of uniting Irishmen by persuasion and in peace, they must get down to hard political thinking. This has been conspicuously lacking in their movement up to the present. They must formulate their political programme in such a way as to make republicanism credible also to unionists as a formula that fully respects and explicitly guarantees the rights and loyalties that distinguish unionism from nationalism. They must declare their readiness to accept unionists as unionists, not as a suppressed minority in a nationalist Ireland. An Ireland predicated on coercion of unionists would be an Ireland that no Irishman with a sense of justice or of patriotism should desire or could accept. It would be an affront to justice. It would be a substitution of one coercion for another. It would be the imposition on a minority in Ireland as a whole of a form of coercion that nationalists are convinced was in the past imposed upon them, a coercion that they believe prepared the ground for the present tragic conflict. Coercion in reverse would merely prepare the way for ongoing chapters of murderous conflict in the future.

If, however, the paramilitary republicans were to call off their campaign of violence, I am convinced that the weariness of violence and the desire for peace among nationalists and unionists are so strong and that the instincts for fairness and justice among Protestants are so genuine that a just settlement could be agreed more quickly than the sceptics believe; it would be a settlement which could offer a new future in peace and in hope to all our children.

## THE CHURCH'S WORD FOR TODAY

The people in Northern Ireland need to have a truly Christian word spoken to them at this time. They need Christian leadership. It is not a question for the Churches of taking political sides but precisely of refusing to take political sides. It is a question rather of taking a stand on the Gospel of Christ. It is a question of testing political options by the standards of the Gospel of Christ.

The Church cannot identify itself with any political community. A Christian preacher speaks to the whole people of God and not to members of the unionist parties or the nationalist parties. The Gospel is for all men, and not just for a politically homogeneous group. The kingdom of God is a universal kingdom, not a political faction. When Churchmen say 'our people', they must not confine the phrase to people of one political persuasion.

It is not good for religion and it is not good for politics in Northern Ireland that to be born in the Protestant faith should automatically mean being born into a unionist or a loyalist political party, and that to be born in the Catholic faith should automatically mean being born into a nationalist or a republican political party. The term 'captivity' has been used by John Morrow to describe the manner in which the Churches have become interlocked with political party allegiances. I wonder how many of us, Catholic or Protestant, have ever found ourselves instinctively feeling that a Catholic or a Protestant has betrayed the Church or compromised the faith when he or she chooses, if a Catholic, not to be nationalist or, if a Protestant, not to be unionist? If this be so, have we not been dangerously confusing the things that are Caesar's with the things that are God's?

We Churchmen must never assert the rights of one community without also affirming the rights of the other community.

In matters where the faith touches on political and social responsibilities, we must not speak out of or to 'our own people' only; we must try to speak for and to the other community as well. To work to reconcile the two communities is our bounden duty as servants of God's universal kingdom of justice, forgiveness, brotherhood, love and peace.

There are many Protestant Churchmen in Northern Ireland who in this time of turmoil and tension have spoken this prophetic word and have been listened to with respect by many in their own community and beyond it. They deserve the admiration and gratitude of all for their courage and integrity. They deserve the support of all for their Christian leadership. One does not exaggerate in comparing their witness to that of the 'Confessing Church' in Hitler's Germany.

The Reformed Churches in particular have in their own tradition the word our society needs to hear, for the Reformed Churches have always stressed the lordship and sovereignty of God over every human institution and all temporal order, and the supremacy of God's Word over every human system of thought and plan of action. It is in the Lord that we Christians find our strength and not in any political tradition. It is our faith and not any political institution that is our victory over the world.

The Protestant and the Catholic communities on this island are bound inextricably together by history, by geography, by economics, by our common Christian name and profession. Our communities are now at a crossroads in our destiny. We can choose the path of reconciliation and collaboration for the good of each community, or we can continue on the road of conflict for the destruction of both communities. As joint participants in this island's history, as fellow sufferers from its conflicts, as fellow sharers in its resources of natural beauty, human goodness and Christian tradition, we must choose the path of reconciliation for this is the path of Christ. In Christ's name, we must be reconciled to one another and therefore to the Lord Our God.

Unionism and nationalism are often presented as totally

47

exclusive of and alien to one another. I suggest that there are broad common principles that any Christian unionist or nationalist must accept. Both unionists and nationalists must unreservedly accept the legitimacy of the opposing viewpoint and the political rights of those who hold that viewpoint. Both must respect the full human and political civic rights, the human dignity and the civic equality of the other, and must resist infringement of those rights, from whatever source they come. Both must be committed to social justice, to equality of opportunity, to fair employment, to rejection of discrimination on political or religious grounds. Both must work for the elimination of injustice and deprivation, in whichever community it be found. Both must strive for the abolition of unemployment and poverty. Both must be committed to the economic recovery of the whole of Northern Ireland so that all its citizens may have a prospect of economic security and job opportunity in this land we all love.

As a Protestant Irish patriot once said, 'Gentlemen, we have a country.' It is a country of which we can all be proud. We must work together to build it up in justice and love, for the benefit of all its citizens. To this end, we put our trust in the Lord, 'whose power, working in us, can do infinitely more than we can ask or even imagine. To Him be glory . . . in the Church and in Christ Jesus, for ages of ages' (Ephesians 3: 20–1).

# 3
## REPUBLICAN VIOLENCE DESTROYS THE WORK OF JUSTICE

*There is no room for ambivalence. In face of the present cam-*
*paigns of republican violence the choice of all Catholics is*
*clear. It is a choice between good and evil.*

*It is sinful to join organisations committed to violence or to*
*remain in them. It is sinful to support such organisations or to*
*call on others to support them . . . People must choose. There is*
*no longer any room for romantic illusion. There is no excuse*
*for thinking that the present violence in Ireland can be morally*
*justified.*

*In face of these recent crimes let us redouble our prayers that*
*the Lord will remove the veil from the eyes of those who will*
*not see and bring about in all hearts a true spirit of repent-*
*ance.* [Statement of the Standing Committee of the Irish Bishops, 9
November 1987]

One most immediate and obvious obstruction to the hope of a
shared Northern Ireland is the campaign of violence being conducted by the IRA and other paramilitary republican groups.

Any intelligent analysis of the Northern problem would demonstrate that there can be no tolerable living for either of our
communities until there is reconciliation between them. Republican paramilitaries speak of 'finishing once and for all the
unfinished business of 1916'. There is indeed unfinished business left from the period 1916 to 1922. It is certainly not military business. It is the business of reconciling the unionist and
nationalist communities in Northern Ireland. It is the business
of evolving a reconciled political arrangement and creating reconciling political institutions that would permit peaceful and
constructive coexistence. These arrangements and these institutions were never before created. It is urgent to create them now.

But violence makes reconciliation between our two communities inordinately difficult. Violence serves – and one must
indeed wonder whether it is intended to serve – to drive our
two communities still further apart.

After twenty-one years of experience of what violence means in practice, the great mass of the people of Ireland, in the Republic as in the North, hold it in utter repugnance and disgust. The claim that a war is being waged in the name and on behalf of the people of Ireland is devoid of all plausibility. Violence has been demasked. Its romantic pretensions, its mythical glory and glamour have been stripped away. The distinction between political crime and 'ordinary crime' has been long ago obliterated, as the alleged glorious 'fight for freedom and justice' takes the form of a succession of inglorious and sordid murders (carefully and coldly planned in advance and carried out with scientific precision), the bombing of so-called economic targets (which has left hundreds of people, both Catholic and Protestant, jobless) and the anti-social fallout that violence of its very nature has caused in the neighbourhoods where it flourishes.

### THE SPIRITUAL DAMAGE DONE BY VIOLENCE

The greatest harm the IRA does to the Catholic community is the spiritual harm it does in weakening the sense of the sacredness and inviolability of human life and in blunting awareness of the awfulness of murder. All sin not only wounds the individual who commits it but also does grave wrong to the Christian community within which it is perpetrated. Particularly frightening is the effect of all this on the moral sense of children and the young. This has fearful consequences for the future of our community. Condemnation of the IRA is not a political but a spiritual matter. The IRA constitutes a grave spiritual danger for sections of the Catholic community. Our Lord said, 'Do not be afraid of those who kill the body, but cannot kill the soul' (Matthew 10: 28). The activities of the IRA are killing the souls of those involved in or actively supporting it. The disgusting graffiti put up by the IRA or their sympathisers after some of their atrocities provide proof of the moral sickness that the so-called armed struggle brings with it.

The Catholic Church through the voice of its bishops and

priests, as well as through the voice of its chief pastor, Pope John Paul II, has repeatedly and most solemnly declared that no one can be a faithful Catholic and at the same time a member of the IRA and similar organisations. No faithful Catholic can claim that there is moral justification for the deeds of violence of these organisations. No one in the name of the Catholic Church can morally condone them. No faithful Catholic can appeal to his or her own conscience as justifying such deeds. All must listen to the words of St Paul: 'My conscience does not condemn me; but that does not mean that I am thereby acquitted. He that judges me is the Lord' (1 Corinthians 4: 4). The Lord alone will be judge of those who disregard the Church teaching in His name. Only the Lord can touch hearts that have been deliberately and systematically hardened against the teaching of His Church.

As for us who are ministers of God's Word, we must and we shall go on proclaiming that Word, unwelcome though it may be to some; we must and we shall go on preaching that message, unpopular though it may be with a few. We shall ourselves be condemned in God's final judgment if we do not preach that Gospel.

The Lord has not guaranteed that everyone will listen to our proclamation of His Word. He has commanded us to go on proclaiming it. We shall ourselves be judged on our fidelity to that command. Every man's and woman's conscience will be judged on whether they have or have not listened. It is God's Word itself that is the judge of every conscience.

I want to plead with the leaders of paramilitary republican organisations and with those who have influence over them. I want to address a direct plea to them, in the name of God and for the honour of the Irish people, to bring the killing to an end. I want to plead with those who joined the organisation in the past for idealistic reasons and out of a passion for justice. I ask them now to have the honesty and the courage to recognise that their involvement has forced them to do and approve of and defend deeds that would have revolted them when they first joined. For God's sake, for Ireland's sake, let them leave the organisation now before still more grievous harm is done to their conscience, to their soul and to our community and our country. Let them turn to peaceful, constructive ways of promoting justice and peace and defending human rights.

To each of you – leader or member of these organisations – I also wish to say, do not ever despair of God's mercy and forgiveness; repent and turn back to God and be reconciled to Him and to the community you have so grievously wronged.

My purpose is not to hurl anathemas at the men and women of the bomb and the bullet. I simply say to you, quietly and confidently: your campaign will never succeed, it can never succeed, for the fundamental reason that it is sinful; and sin is already defeated, its seeming success is trumpery, its apparent power is illusion. It is as true now as when St Paul spoke that 'where sin increased, grace abounded all the more' (Romans 5: 21). To the men and women of the bomb and the bullet I wish to speak quietly and lovingly: no matter what you do, you will never succeed in making God stop loving you and waiting for you to turn away from your sins so that He may forgive you. Wherever you hide, His love will find you, His grace will wait at your door. Your consciences will never give you peace until you open the door to Him and ask for His forgiveness.

THE SECTARIAN ASPECT OF REPUBLICAN VIOLENCE

The republican movement professes the objective of uniting Protestant and Catholic in a non-sectarian Ireland. How demented, how self-contradictory their methods of uniting Ireland are has been made most brutally clear by a series of murders of Protestants perpetrated especially in the counties adjoining the border with the Republic.

No amount of protestation that these persons were murdered not because they were Protestants but because they were members of British security forces can remove, or should be expected to remove, the conviction of Protestant communities, especially along the border, that there is a republican policy to exterminate them, or at least to force them to leave their homes.

Protestations to the contrary may be sincerely meant. Republican killers may not see themselves as sectarian killers. But there is no way that the reality of what they have done could have been perceived by the Protestant communities in question otherwise than as sectarian killings. Those who planned these murders would seem to believe that the taint of sectarian killing will be removed by the occasional murder of Catholic members of the security forces. But this proves nothing except how insane and evil is the logic of the present IRA. It merely proves that violence perverts reason and corrupts logic.

The greatest proportion of British security forces now operating in Northern Ireland are Northern Irish. By far the largest proportion of all victims of republican killings in recent years have been Irishmen. They have for the most part been unionists, acting naturally and logically in accordance with unionist principles. Milkmen have been killed on their peaceful milk rounds, postmen delivering letters, bus drivers driving children's buses, fathers before their wives and children, policemen helping schoolchildren across the road, policemen giving traffic directions. Unionist politicians have been killed. British politicians have been killed. Killings such as these could not escape being called murders of opposing politicians simply because of their political views. Indeed they could not but be perceived as sectarian murders of Protestants because they are Protestants. Such actions are a betrayal of historical republicanism.

Sinn Féin and IRA spokesmen frequently reiterate their commitment to respect the rights of Protestants and unionists in the future united Irish Republic for which they claim to struggle. That pledge of future respect is directly contradicted by present performance. Fratricide between Irishmen now is not a means towards brotherhood between Irishmen later. Present practice is a total negation of future promise.

But even in the present policy statements of the Sinn Féin/IRA version of republicanism, the rights of Protestants are by definition limited. These statements make it clear that Protestants will be granted every right except the right to be unionists. Unionists will have full equality of rights with other Irish men and women when and if they become Irish nationalists. Unless and until they do so, they have no rightful place in the Irish nation and cannot share in the Sinn Féin 'charter of rights' for a 'post-partition, independent Ireland'.

This has only to be stated for it to be made manifest how utterly it contradicts fundamental civil rights and also how divorced it is from reality and political realism. It is a recipe for the denial to unionists by nationalists of the very same civil rights that were denied to nationalists by unionists in the past.

THE DENIAL OF THE RIGHT TO LIFE

The campaign of violence is not the pursuit of civil rights by other means. It is the destruction of civil rights, not only for unionists but also for nationalists. It is a campaign of repression. It is counter-reformist and indeed, in the proper sense of the term, counter-revolutionary.

The most basic of all civil rights is the right to life; the IRA denies the right to life to whole categories of people whom its leaders choose at any particular time to name 'legitimate targets'; these categories seem indefinitely revisable and expandable according to the shifting moods of the planners of death, or according to the publicity potential of the 'operation', or even simply according as opportunities for killings present themselves.

The fact is that more civilians than members of the security forces have been killed in the Troubles, and a majority of the civilians killed have been Catholics. A campaign purporting to be waged against British occupying forces has killed or maimed many times more natives of this island than it has members of the British Army. All these murders and maimings are equally evil and deplorable. There are no legitimate targets. There is no acceptable level of 'civilian casualties'. The statistics of the murdered and the maimed make a nonsense of the claim that the IRA campaign is an Irish national struggle for freedom from foreign British occupation.

SOCIAL JUSTICE

Paramilitary republicans present their campaign of violence as the only way to the liberation of the most deprived sections of the Northern nationalist community from deprivation, oppression, discrimination, and harassment by security forces. It is preponderantly on these grounds that they obtain such limited support as they receive. It is strange that they do not see, and sad that some others do not see, that paramilitary violence only increases deprivation, deepens economic depression, and provokes security forces harassment. It is the nationalist community that suffers most from paramilitary republicanism. It is Catholic communities that are its first casualties.

Some republican activists undeniably have a social conscience and a commitment to justice. But the nature of guerrilla activity is such that it is the community out of which it operates that pays the price. It is the innocent who suffer.

Paramilitary operations lead by contagion to all sorts of anti-social behaviour. They produce a run-down and demoralising environment. All this is the very opposite of liberation. Violence, once it is unleashed, cannot be switched off at will. Its momentum carries over into crime and lawlessness, destruction and joyriding and vandalism. One dimension of paramilitary activity has become so common that it escapes almost unnoticed and unreported. Scarcely a month passes without the admission of young men to hospital with severe injuries to head and limbs and with bodies bruised all over, after being viciously battered on head and arms and legs by hooded men with hurley sticks and wooden staves, allegedly for 'anti-social behaviour'. The barbaric behaviour of such 'punishment squads' is a measure of the degradation of moral standards and the debasement of the quality of life that IRA violence has inflicted on some communities. Robberies, hijackings, kidnappings and protection rackets as well as being immoral in themselves, all produce a disastrous debasing of moral standards. Drinking clubs associated with paramilitary organisations are a source of grave abuse and demoralisation. Children whom paramilitaries have trained in the tactics of street rioting will be very prone to use the same tactics to terrorise whole neighbourhoods and to make life unbearable for the inhabitants, and especially the old.

It is undeniable that crime, marital breakdown, family neglect are all much more prevalent in Catholic areas now than they were before the advent of the so-called armed struggle for their liberation. These effects may not be directly intended by the republican paramilitaries. But they are the inseparable consequences of their campaign.

'Destabilisation' is a favourite word of paramilitary republicans. But it is not British institutions or official Northern Ireland institutions or unionist institutions that are being destabilised. It is Catholic communities, Catholic parishes, that are the most exposed to the effects of destabilisation. Marriage and family life in the affected areas suffer grievously. Part of the toll of paramilitarism is broken homes and uncontrollable children. Paramilitaries must agonise over the effect of their way of life on their own marriages and their own children. They should agonise also over the effects of their campaign on the families and children of their fellow nationalists. But these effects are the inevitable result of their campaign and cannot be remedied while the campaign rages. Republicans speak of a brave new Ireland to arise from the ashes after the guns are laid aside. But the new Ireland is being created already by the physical force campaign, and it is an Ireland that the vast majority of Irish people, North and South, find totally alien to their history and their values.

EVIL MEANS

The IRA campaign has conditioned its members into believing that what would ordinarily be murder is not murder when carried out in a 'war situation', or for the sake of 'the Cause', or in obedience to 'Army orders'. With strong and repeated emphasis, Pope John Paul condemned this evil doctrine during his visit to Ireland. In Drogheda, he said:

> I pray with you that the moral sense and Christian conviction of Irish men and women may never become obscured and blunted by the lie of violence, that nobody may ever call murder by any other name than murder, that the spiral of violence may never

be given the distinction of unavoidable logic or necessary retaliation. [*The Pope in Ireland*, p. 21]

In the course of his great prayer of trust and consecration of Ireland to Mary, the Mother of God, in Knock, he said:

> Teach us all that evil means can never lead to a good end; that all human life is sacred; that murder is murder no matter what the motive or end. [Homily at Knock, 30 September 1979, in *The Pope in Ireland*, p. 56]

Indeed, it is a foundation principle of all authentic morality that one may never do a morally evil thing in order to obtain a good result. Contrarily, it is a feature of all apologias for immorality that good intentions and good consequences are held to justify the doing of evil things. It has, however, become a cardinal principle of the philosophy and the ethics of terrorism everywhere that any and every means are held to be justified, so long as they are intended, or are judged to be effective, towards bringing about a good result. This theory, as well as being radically immoral, is a direct contradiction of the theology of the just war.

## JUST WAR THEOLOGY

'Thou shall not kill', 'human life is sacred': however formulated, the moral principle of the sacredness of human life is one of the foundation principles of the moral patrimony of humanity. Although one must be careful about imputing moral decline to a historical epoch, it seems doubtful whether any age has seen such damaging blows delivered to this principle, both in thinking and in practice, as our own age. The twentieth century has undoubtedly seen more violent and man-inflicted death, more cruelty of man to man, more torture, more repression, more exploitation, than any previous century. The record of this century challenges the belief that moral progress is a normal by-product of development in education, in science and in technology.

Indeed, the record challenges our very use of the term 'development' and its derivatives. Our common use of the term carries the emotive flavour of moral approval for the industrially and technologically developed nations. But the industrially developed countries manifest grave symptoms of moral underdevelopment. Our habitual use of the term 'developed countries' can be insulting to the Third World, and can embody a very muddled sort of moral thinking.

The moral underdevelopment of much of the industrially developed world is not only a matter of actual moral practice. It is manifested by a crisis of moral thinking, of moral discussion, of moral language; indeed, a crisis of values.

Contemporary discussion regarding the morality of killing reflects much of the modern confusion in moral thinking. The traditional moral reasoning about the just war is much more coherent and realistic, as well as more morally enlightened and compassionate. This tradition is too often dismissed summarily nowadays without being thoroughly examined or correctly understood. After all, a great and truly liberal thinker like Jacques Maritain could say that the theologians and moralists of the just war tradition 'perform a work of mercy, enabling us to live on this earth'.

A common misunderstanding of the just war theology is that its aim was to justify war or violence. This is not so. Its central affirmation is to declare that war, violence, killing are immoral – except in certain extreme conditions. Indeed, for this theology the killing of the innocent is intrinsically evil, and there are no exceptions. The extreme conditions mentioned above presuppose a situation in which certain people have forfeited their description as 'innocent' because of unjust aggression of a grievous kind against the fundamental human rights of others, and in which there exists no way of defending those rights other than the use of self-defensive violence. The presumption in this tradition always was that war and other forms of killing are evil. There must be absolutely compelling reasons to set aside this presumption and to hold war in certain circumstances to be justified.

Even when these conditions were held to be fulfilled and war was allowed to be in certain circumstances justified, stringent conditions were postulated governing the methods and the weapons whose use was morally permissible, even in a war held to be just in principle. To give moral approval or condonation to war was never to approve of any and every means of waging that war. Side by side with the theology of the just war went an unceasing effort, all through the medieval period, to limit the destructiveness of war, to control the bloodlust of the combatants, to outlaw the more lethal and cruel of the weapons, and to insist that they be used only against combatants, and never against non-combatants or innocent civilians. All kinds of limitations and controls were proposed by theologians, promulgated by the Church, embodied in treaties and adopted into the corpus of international law. These conventions have been progressively flouted in modern times, which have seen an increasing use of indiscriminate weapons of death, destruction and terror.

For example, no exponent of just war theology ever could justify by its principles the German bombing of British cities or the Allied 'carpet bombing' of German cities or the atom bombs dropped on Hiroshima and Nagasaki. It was, paradoxically, 'liberal' Churchmen who supplied moral whitewash for a use of atom bombs. Revd Joseph Fletcher, for example, justified it on the basis of 'situation ethics', or the 'new morality' of love (Revd Joseph Fletcher, *Situation Ethics: the new morality*, SCM Press, 1966, p. 98). He declared that it was 'on a vast scale of agapeic calculus' that the decision of President Truman to drop atom bombs was based. It is strange what 'love' can be held to justify when the scale is sufficiently vast! It is, however, impossible to appeal to the just war tradition in support of an argument of this kind. The just war theology, to repeat, was designed not to justify war but rather to prevent war or, when this proved impossible, to restrict its savagery and destructiveness.

But when the state of technology and the breakdown of the Christian moral consensus combine to make these efforts at restriction more and more unrealistic and irrelevant, the time has come to ask whether there are in fact any situations of war or revolution now in which the conditions for a just war or a just revolution could be verified. I believe that the theology of the just war is still valid in principle; but I see it as more and more difficult to verify its conditions in the modern practice of either war or revolution. *De facto* a mystique and a methodology of war and of revolution have developed, in which indiscriminate and almost uncontrolled destruction and death can be wreaked and, at one and the same time, any and every degree of destruction, death and terror are held to be just and morally right as means, so long as the end is passionately held to be desirable.

Theorists of revolution are now almost openly advocating in theory and adopting in practice a philosophy of utter moral indifference in respect of means of destruction and tactics of terror. The just war theology never regarded the means used as morally indifferent, once the end could be held just. Indeed, this traditional theology had a radically different view of ends and means in morals. The traditional view was that the end is embodied in the means and that to will evil means is already to infect the end with the same moral evil.

The past twenty-one years of violence in the North of Ireland provide a laboratory demonstration of the evils of revolutionary violence in modern conditions. These tragic years provide conclusive demonstration of the truth of Pope John Paul's warning that violence creates greater evils and greater injustices than those it set out to eradicate. The ends desired by the revolutionaries have long ago been contradicted by the means they have used. The present campaign of violence in Northern Ireland stands condemned by the principles of the just war theology that it invokes. There is no moral justification for the use of violence to advance any political cause in Ireland at this time.

If resort to and continuation of violence in Ireland is immoral, this is not a refutation of the theology of the just war. It is rather an exemplification of the validity of its basic principles. Every single condition for the just war or the just revolution is violated in the Irish situation. If we wish in future to demonstrate that violence does not work, that violence is not an acceptable or an effective means of promoting justice, we will be able to point to the North of Ireland in the 1970s and 1980s. It is infinitely tragic, however, for a community to be made the captive object of such a cruel vivisection.

I believe that it is mistaken to overstress the contrast between the just war tradition and the pacifist tradition. The just war theology was subtended by a basically pacifist or non-violent spirituality and morality; it was situated in a context of what we might call presumptive pacifism. Its criteria for distinguishing just from unjust wars were designed to ensure that this presumption could yield only to extreme circumstances and under stringent restrictions. The thrust of just war theology was to prevent wars, not to justify them.

One of the classic exponents of just war theology was Aquinas. In his *Summa Theologica* (II/II, question 40, article 1) he said that in reference to the morality of war, the questions that have to be asked are as follows:

1. Is the decision to wage war taken by the competent authority, who alone can commit a collectivity to war?

2. Is the cause of war a just one? That is to say, is the war a necessary response to the infliction of grave injustice? Differently put, is recourse to war the last recourse, embarked upon only when all means of peaceful solution have been exhausted?

3. Is the intention morally right? In other words, is the war-like action directed towards the restoration of justice and peace, and therefore towards the re-establishment of the order of love which should reign between men and nations?

Later authors in the just war tradition expanded these conditions into what might be called a 'principle of proportionality'. They insisted that, not only must the original decision to go to war be morally justified, but the means of waging war that are adopted must be proportionate to the injustice suffered, must not be a source of new injustice, and must be compatible with the overall intention to re-establish the order of justice, reconciliation and peace.

The subsequent development of this thomistic treatment of the just war was indebted also to Aquinas's discussion of the right to and the limits of self-defence, and to his absolute moral exclusion of the 'unjust killing of the innocent'. Regarding self-defence, he required that the degree of force used must be no greater than is necessary and sufficient to repel the aggressor and to avert the crime. For example, one may not kill an aggressor except in defence of one's life or of some incommutable value. The unjust killing of the innocent, however, is intrinsically and unconditionally and always gravely immoral.

I turn now to the moral evaluation, in the light of the just war theology, of the present self-styled 'armed struggle' of paramilitary republicanism.

First, this fails the test of 'competent authority' to commit a country or a people to war. The so-called war is claimed to be waged on behalf of the Irish people. Against this, it must be said first of all that this claim defines nearly 1 million unionist Irish men and women as non-people. The claim is refuted also by the fact that all but a tiny minority of the nationalist people in Ireland as a whole reject the use of physical force to advance nationalist aspirations and repudiate the pretension of a small and unrepresentative faction to speak and act in their name.

Furthermore, even in the North of Ireland, it is under false pretences that Sinn Féin claim votes for their party as a mandate for the armalite. It is frankly dishonest to appeal for votes in support of political and cultural and social and local community aims and then claim that those votes are votes for violence. At election times Sinn Féin leaders and canvassers regularly assure voters that a vote for Sinn Féin is not to be understood as a vote for violence. After the election, however, all votes registered for Sinn Féin are claimed as a mandate for the armed struggle. If electoral support for the IRA's paramilitary campaign were openly and honestly sought, it would become clear to the world how little support or sympathy for violence exists in the nationalist community.

The 'just cause' criterion must next be examined. That there has been and is injustice in Northern Ireland, both in the structures

64

of government and in the practice of administration and in the distribution of social and economic opportunity, is undeniable. I wish that fair-minded unionists would recognise how deeply hurtful and how unjust it is to a community of nearly 600,000 people to be denied full and equal citizenship in their own country unless they change their political party. It is surely inconsistent to expect nationalists to accept in Northern Ireland a status that unionists vehemently reject and refuse for themselves in a united Ireland. The claims and aspirations of democratic nationalists are no threat to unionists. They are a threat only to an inequality of rights, which makes society unstable for unionism itself. Indeed, the commitment to pursue nationalist aims only by peaceful and democratic means is a greater threat to paramilitary republicanism than it is to unionism.

The only acceptable future for both our communities lies in reconciliation between them, each retaining its own identity and its political and civil rights yet each accepting the other in its differences, and each conceding the other's rights. The need for political change must be accepted, so that neither community will dominate the other or seek to impose its particular political philosophy on the other. Individuals must be reconciled. Communities must be reconciled. We Church leaders have our responsibility, and history will not forgive us if we shirk it. Politicians have a special responsibility. Unless there are constitutional arrangements favouring reconciliation, exhortation alone will never bring it about. There must be reconciled and reconciling institutions as well as reconciling and reconciled people. This is what justice in the Northern Ireland situation means.

The republican paramilitary campaign is totally incompatible with that justice. It rests on a radically mistaken political analysis of the situation. Of its very nature, it drives the communities further apart. How could any rational being see this as a way forward to a united Ireland?

POLARISATION

Paramilitary campaigns can be sustained only if passions are kept constantly inflamed and hatred enkindled. Pope John Paul has said:

> Passions are sometimes fed deliberately. It is difficult for wars to start if the people on both sides do not have powerful feelings of mutual hostility, or if they are not convinced that the claims of their opponents threaten their vital interests. This explains the ideological manipulations resorted to by those with aggressive intentions. Once fighting has begun, hostility is bound to increase, for it is nourished by the sufferings and atrocities experienced by each side. Psychoses of hatred can then result.
> [Message for World Day of Peace, 1 January 1984]

In both our communities, many are imprisoned by memories of past wrongs and injustices, suffered and inflicted. We are captives of our past and we cannot liberate ourselves from that past by our own unaided efforts. We remain so locked within that hurt past that we inflict on our own community and on what we call 'the other community' misery in the present and hopelessness about our future.

The prejudices are deep. The suspicions are of long standing. The way forward will not be easy. No one formula for a solution is sure to succeed. But one proposed 'solution' is sure to fail: namely the solution of violence. It is sure to fail because it contradicts the end it sets itself to achieve. By the terms of the just war tradition it is immoral. The minority community in Northern Ireland can never succeed by the way of violence. People like Ghandi, Martin Luther King, Lech Walesa show that it is non-violence that is the weapon of those who are physically weak but morally strong and is the true path to justice.

To the men and women committed to violence, all Christians, Catholic and Protestant, should say quietly and lovingly in the spirit of Martin Luther King: 'No matter what you do, you will not succeed in making us hate each other, or regard "the other community" as enemy, as alien, or disloyal or as not belonging.'

VIOLENCE AND POLITICS INCOMPATIBLE

It is a disastrous mistake to regard constitutional nationalism as merely physical force republicanism carried on by other means. Constitutional nationalists detest violence as much as unionists do. They seek only a land where both Irish communities can work together to restore our devastated economy, to create prospects of jobs for our young people and to give us all hope for our future in the land we all love and wish to share. This is a task to challenge both unionist loyalty and nationalist patriotism. We face it together in partnership or we destroy it separately by short-sighted and self-destructive intransigence.

I make bold to say that nothing would more quickly and effectively discredit paramilitary republicanism than a declaration from unionist leaders that they are open to reasonable political change and to accommodation with constitutional nationalism. Unionist refusal of change is perhaps the paramilitaries' chief propaganda and their principal source of support. Moderates in unionist circles must bring their influence to bear on their leaders to enter into openminded discussion with democratic nationalists, so that institutions can be evolved that fully safeguard unionist rights but which can also win the assent of the nationalist community. Courageous individuals of unionist persuasion, in many walks of life and in the media, have striven valiantly for new thinking in their community. They should know that very many, both Catholics and Protestants, admire their integrity and hope that they will persevere, in face of opposition and in spite of rebuffs, in their honourable task. They are doing a true work of reconciliation. As Christians, they will know that reconciliation passes by the way of the Cross. Non-unionists who defend the rights of unionists and who denounce paramilitary violence are risking unpopularity for the sake of truth and principle. It is time for a positive reponse from the unionist leadership.

## FUTILITY OF VIOLENCE

Violence must, after a cruel twenty-one years' experience, be pronounced morally and politically bankrupt. It has not advanced an inch towards achieving any of its stated objectives. It has led its adherents into actions of which they would at the outset have thought themselves incapable, and which indeed some of its early leaders must surely now deplore. Of all the methods available for securing a solution to our problems, violence is demonstrably the only one that cannot succeed and never will succeed. Its unavoidable consequences are the exact opposite of its stated intentions.

There is no possibility of justice until the physical force campaign has been called off. The powerlessness of violence to achieve justice has been conclusively proved. The power of non-violent action for justice has not yet been really tried. The lesson of Poland's Solidarity movement and of its non-violent struggle for justice and freedom should be studied and applied to Ireland. In face of one of the most powerful and most repressive police regimes in the world, Solidarity secured by non-violent means the dismantling of the oppressive regime itself and the establishment of human rights, freedoms and social justice that could in no other way have been secured. Powerful states can respond to violence only too effectively by greater violence. What they do not know how to cope with is non-violent action by a disciplined and united community.

If the physical force campaign were called off, polarisation between our two communities would lessen rapidly and moderate opinion would be able to assert itself and exert pressure for peace and justice. World opinion could be mobilised to press for just political solutions to the Irish problem. European and American money would certainly be made available for reconstruction. There could be a commitment by both the British and Irish governments to switch the monies now absorbed by security into the rehabilitation of the most afflicted areas and the creation of jobs, with guarantees of fair employment, for both communities. Unemployment, now running at calamitous levels, especially in nationalist areas, housing conditions often unworthy of human dignity, particularly in blocks of flats, deprivation in its multiple forms all create conditions conducive to alienation and violence. But the violence only aggravates them. New housing, environmental rehabilitation, large-scale industrial investment and developments are crying needs. But violence obstructs and deters them. It delays the day of social justice.

The futility of physical force is now glaringly evident. I have no doubt but that Padraig Pearse would long ago have called off the campaign, as he did on the Saturday of Easter Week 1916, 'in order to prevent further slaughter of citizens'. The signatories of the Republican Proclamation of Easter 1916 said: 'We pray that no one who serves [the cause of the Irish Republic] will dishonour it by . . . inhumanity or rapine.' What would they have said about La Mon, Abercorn, Darkley, the Birmingham pub bombings, the bombing at Harrods of Christmas shoppers, the Enniskillen bomb, the killing of three RUC constables at Armagh and the concomitant slaughter by the same landmine of Sister Catherine Dunn – which the IRA had the indecency and vulgarity to call 'a fluke'? James Connolly would certainly never have countenanced the continuation of a campaign that divided Protestant and Catholic workers and regarded Protestant working men as 'legitimate targets' and bombed so-called economic targets, leaving working-class Catholics and Protestants jobless.

REPUDIATION OF VIOLENCE

In June 1986 a group of Protestant and Catholic clergy and laity joined together in publishing a *Declaration of Faith and Commitment by Christians in Northern Ireland*. Together they declared:

> We believe that all our land belongs to God: not to Unionists or Nationalists. All of us have to live in and share it together . . .
> Our differences are no excuse for refusing to seek reconciliation with God and with each other . . . [Section 1, p. 2]

Catholics and Protestants must submit the sincerity of their repudiation of violence to a test: do we consciously or half-consciously make a distinction between 'our' paramilitaries and 'their' paramilitaries? Do we find ourselves saying that violence coming from 'our' community is somehow understandable, unavoidable, the only argument 'they' will listen to, the only method that gets results? Let our rejection of violence be absolute and total. 'No' is a familiar cry in Northern Ireland's past history and our present experience. Let our loudest 'No' be said to all use of violence and all threat of violence. Let that 'No' be unqualified, without conditions and without exceptions. In the words of the declaration, 'We reject the lie that justice can be achieved by the use of violence' (ibid.).

JUSTICE

Rejection of violence is imperative, but it is not enough. We must be committed to work for justice, justice not just for 'our own community', but justice for both communities. Let us again apply a test to our concern for justice. Do we care as much about justice for 'the other community' as we do about our own? Do the great social evils of unemployment and the related problem of emigration disturb us more when they affect 'our own community' than when they affect 'the others'? God sees us as His sons and daughters, made in His own image, remade in the image of His Son. St Paul says:

> In that image there is no room for distinction between Greek and Jew, between the circumcised and the uncircumcised, or between barbarian and Scythian, slave and free man. There is only Christ: he is everything and he is in everything. [Colossians 3:11]

RECONCILIATION

Violence makes the work of reconciliation humanly more difficult. But reconciliation is not a merely human task: it is a divine work, an already accomplished fact, a present reality. St Paul says:

> It is all God's work. It was God who reconciled us to Himself through Christ and gave us the work of handing on this reconciliation . . . God in Christ was reconciling the world to Himself . . . and He has entrusted to us the news that they are reconciled. [2 Corinthians 5: 18–19]

Who can set us free to love and forgive one another, and thus open up a new future for both of our communities? Only Jesus Christ, Our Lord. He announced himself at the beginning of his mission as the one who was sent from heaven

> to proclaim liberty to captives
> and to the blind new sight.
> [Luke 4: 18]

When Jesus had called Lazarus from death to life he said, 'Unbind him; let him go free' (John 11: 44). May our prayers be that both communities in our country hear the call of Our Lord to shake off the bonds of hate and prejudice and walk free into a new future of peace and mutual respect. This is what our faith in Christ can do. This is what the love of Christ can do. There may be mountains of prejudice and bigotry confronting and surrounding us. But faith in Christ can move those mountains.

We must pray for those who within the Catholic community exploit hatred and resentment and revenge, that they and the whole Catholic community may see that these attitudes are opposed to everything the Catholic Church stands for, everything she has learned from her Lord. Nothing could be more destructive of a Catholic community than hatred. It is a betrayal of our faith. It is a corruption of the community of faith and love that we are called to be. We are the people who 'have put our faith in love' (1 John 4: 16), and to desert the way of love for the ways of hate and murder is to walk away from Christ.

In the words of the votive Mass for times of civil disturbance we pray:

> God our Father,
> maker and lover of peace,
> to know you is to live;
> and to serve you is to reign.
> All our faith is in your saving help;
> protect us from men of violence
> and keep us safe from weapons of hate.

71

And we invoke the intercession of Mary, Queen of Peace.

We take refuge in your protection
O holy Mother of God.
Do not despise our prayers
in our time of need
but deliver us always from all dangers
O ever glorious and blessed Virgin.

# 4
## THE SECTARIAN FACTOR
## IN LOYALISM

*In our time, when so many innocent people are perishing at the hands of others, the biblical description of what happened between Cain and Abel becomes particularly eloquent . . . Does not that question of God's addressed to Cain 'Where is your brother?' speak to us even more than the absolute ban 'not to kill'. And following up closely on Cain's evasive reply, 'Am I my brother's keeper?' comes the other divine question: 'What have you done? The voice of your brother's blood is crying to me from the ground!'* [Pope John Paul II, Letter of Gratitude, written during his convalescence after an assassination attempt, 8 December 1981]

GRIM REALITY OF SECTARIAN KILLING

The struggle in Northern Ireland has dragged on now for so long that only the more horrific outrages receive substantial coverage in the media. The individual killings that happen virtually every week merit only a paragraph or two in the British press. Even in Ireland, last week's killings are forgotten this week. Yet each murderous bullet carries with it an immense weight of human heartbreak.

In the homes of all the victims, there is found the same grief and shock and bewilderment, the same distressed parents and heartbroken widows and crying, terrified and uncomprehending children. Behind each unit of the grim statistics of casualties there lies a personal and family tragedy.

Public attention has understandably focused on the role of the IRA and other paramilitary republican groups in perpetrating these murders and causing the associated personal and family tragedy. It should also be emphasised that there has been a horrifying parallel campaign of sectarian killings by loyalists; indeed retaliatory murders of random Catholics in revenge for IRA killing have been part of the loyalist terrorist tradition for many generations. A typical loyalist terrorist reaction to any IRA atrocity is to kill any convenient Catholic, since any Catholic, in their perverted mentality, is a suspect terrorist. Indeed, anyone encountered in a Catholic area is a presumptive 'legitimate target' for assassination.

The statistics of sectarian killings are truly horrifying. In the past twenty-one years over 500 innocent Catholics have been murdered by loyalist sectarian killers: in other words, murdered for no other reason than that they were Catholics. There have been 53 such murders in the diocese of Down and Connor alone in my eight years as Bishop. I have personally officiated at the funerals of 40 such victims in these eight years. These victims are selected for killing for no other reason than that they are Catholics; that, in itself, in the eyes of loyalist paramilitaries, makes them suspect terrorists or sympathisers with terrorists.

SECTARIAN INTIMIDATION

Sectarian intimidation of Catholics is another unfortunate feature of the Northern Ireland conflict for many generations now. One of the events that decisively affected and continues to affect our continuing tragedy was the campaign of sectarian intimidation in the early 1970s, which drove some 10,000 families, or something like 40,000 people, from their homes. The great majority of these were Catholics. A significant proportion of the present crowded Catholic population of west Belfast comprises families driven from their homes and streets by loyalist gangs at that period. While I am deeply edified by the remarkable lack of bitterness that I find among the immense majority of these Catholic families and among the Catholic population in general, it would be idle to deny that those experiences of the early 1970s continue to be a factor in the alienation of many in west Belfast.

Several Protestant clergy have strongly condemned attacks upon Catholic churches and schools and upon Catholic families. Many have publicly and privately tendered sympathy to the clergy and communities and the individual families affected by these attacks, and to myself personally. I wish here to express my admiration for their Christian stand and my appreciation of their solidarity and fellowship.

It must be firmly stated that people who perpetrate these acts are not typical of the Protestant community. In many cases they have little if any association with any Protestant Church. Their conception of Protestantism has little to do with religious faith and much to do with ethnic or tribal identity and a primitive concept of territoriality. This is a distortion of Christianity. It is a perversion of Protestantism. Quite often, the perpetrators of sectarian attacks are people who are availing of a situation of tension and communal unrest to give vent to violent propensities that would be likely in other circumstances to be expressed in terms of other forms of violence. We must all be careful not to engage in ascription of communal guilt. Our society has suffered too much from a disposition to blame a whole community for the sins of an unrepresentative few. Catholics, who have suffered so much from the imputation to them of collective guilt or guilt by association, should be the last to engage in this despicable practice themselves.

Catholics themselves should feel shame at the isolated instances of sectarian violence that have been committed by persons from within the Catholic community. Those guilty of attacks against Protestant property or homes or persons bring disgrace upon the Catholic community. We must pray for them, that they may have the grace to repent of these sinful deeds and come to see how grievously their behaviour contradicts their Catholic faith and Catholic name, and how shamefully they offend against the first and greatest of God's Commandments, that we must love our neighbour as we love our own self.

SECTARIAN POLITICS

Some politicians during the last twenty-one years have been guilty of a sinister series of expressions of sectarian attitudes; for example, there was a blacklisting of persons with Catholic names working in the media, which fortunately led to an apology by the chairperson of the Ulster Unionist Council. There were damaging remarks about Catholics working in the civil service. There has been a disgraceful suggestion that Catholic nurses from the Republic were 'probably sympathisers with the killing campaign of IRA terrorists'.

Sadly it must be added also that there are pulpits in this land of ours from which a weekly torrent of polluted propaganda is poured out against the Catholic Church. There are few places left in the Western world where any Christian pastors preach prejudice and lies and hatred in respect of their fellow Christians. All of us, Catholics and Protestants alike, must be deeply concerned that Northern Ireland is prominent among these very few places. We must pray and work, Catholics and Protestants together, to show that such behaviour has no place in our understanding of Christianity. As Christians, we cannot rest until this curse of sectarianism is banished from our land.

We must call for the repudiation of all speeches inciting to inter-community violence, and for the retraction of speeches in this vein that have already been uttered. It is necessary to ask whether Article 13 of the Public Order (Northern Ireland) Order of 1981, dealing with incitement to hatred, does not need to be revised and made really effective and to be made operative.

Sectarianism in politics is, alas, not only verbal. There are local councillors, one of whose main concerns seems to be to fight tooth and nail against any real or imagined benefit for Catholics or nationalists, whether in housing, education, social amenities, jobs or in any other domain. It is true that unionist political representatives have been murdered by the IRA, and that others are on what is deplorably called the 'legitimate target list' of the IRA. This has to have an influence on unionist attitudes. Nevertheless, violence is not lessened by adding one more twist to its vicious spiral of hate.

Sectarianism is a disgrace to a community of Christians. Protestant sectarianism is as great a danger to the Protestantism it claims to defend as to the Catholicism it sees as the enemy. It is a contradiction of the true ethos of Protestant Christianity.

We must pray that hatred and prejudice may be replaced by

love, mutual acceptance and respect. We must pray that those who foment sectarian bigotry may be recognised for what they are: enemies of authentic Protestantism, as much as, perhaps more than, enemies of Catholicism. For they preach a word which is not the Word that God wishes to speak to our society at this time. They substitute an anti-Gospel of hatred for Christ's Gospel of freedom from hate and liberation into love.

SECTARIAN ATTACKS

The sectarian dimension of the Northern Ireland Troubles is vividly demonstrated by reference to several specific Catholic parishes, in east Belfast, and along the Shore Road.

The first is St Anthony's, Willowfield, in east Belfast. The mere presence of Catholics here was resented and opposed by bigoted fundamentalist Protestants and by extremist loyalists from the earliest days of the eastward expansion of Belfast and the arrival of Catholics from country districts to work in the early industrial plants established there. East Belfast was claimed to be Protestant territory, which Catholics had no right to enter. The issue of the magazine the *Ulster Protestant* for November 1938, the month following the dedication of the new St Anthony's Church, attacked what it called the 'dumping of Papists' from west and north Belfast into Willowfield, which, the magazine alleged, would now be planned, in order to 'hold' the 'captured' area for the Papacy!

In the event, things were to take an exact opposite turn. The next forty years were to see instead a series of sectarian pogroms, leading to the mass expulsion of Catholics from Willowfield into west Belfast and elsewhere. These pogroms against Catholics have been a recurring feature of the history of east Belfast. They reached a climax in the 1920s and again in the mid-1930s. The plan to build a new Catholic church in Willowfield was ready for implementation in the 1920s. It had to be postponed because of anti-Catholic riots; the money collected for the purpose was handed over instead for emergency relief for refugees. The decision to proceed with the building in the years 1935 to 1938 was an act of exceptional courage on the part of bishop, priests and people. The building operation was marred by many ugly manifestations of sectarian hate. When the new church building was nearly completed, two landmines in succession were planted on the site a few months before the dedication date. The building was narrowly saved from destruction.

Following the dedication of St Anthony's Church in 1938, there was comparative calm in the area until the early 1970s. In 1972 and the years following, sectarian hatred intensified. Catholics in their hundreds were terrorised out of Willowfield and driven into west Belfast or further afield, to Downpatrick or elsewhere. Within three years some 400 families left. In one three-week period 60 families departed. In October 1972 and again in February 1973, gangs of youths and adults attacked the church and the presbytery in a frenzied orgy of destruction, wrecking everything that could be reached and smashed and finally attempting to set both the church and the house on fire. Among the saddest photographs from the whole of the present Troubles are those showing the devastation of the interior of St Anthony's. One is particularly poignant; it shows the parish priest of St Anthony's, the late Father John Courtney, sitting amid the desolation of his church, surrounded by the broken pieces of smashed statues and crucifixes and shattered Stations of the Cross and by upturned and wrecked benches.

St Anthony's parish was brought near to the brink of extinction. The population declined from 2,700 in 1970 to 600 in 1974. By 1976, it was as low as 500. Today it is about 465. The decline in the school population is even more alarming. From 480 pupils in January 1971, the numbers fell to less than half that number in the next three years. In January 1975, the total enrolment was 131. The decline continued to the point where there are now only about 51 pupils in the parish primary school. Very few young people or young families remain in this once vibrant and growing parish. The church, built fifty years ago for an expanding population, now has only a remnant of its former congregation.

Another group of parishes similarly illustrates the scale and intensity of anti-Catholic violence, this time along the Shore Road. I refer to the parishes of Whitehouse, Whiteabbey, Greencastle and that part of the parish of Carrickfergus that is Greenisland. Between 1969 and the mid-1970s, sectarian intimidation and violence forced about 1,500 Catholic families in this group of parishes from their homes. Catholics along the whole Shore Road area were affected. Loyalists, carrying lists of names and addresses of Catholic residents, systematically attacked Catholic homes one by one, smashing windows and doors, bursting into living-rooms, wrecking and threatening. Within a few weeks, in some cases overnight, new Protestant tenants were in possession of the vacated houses. The new parochial house in Greencastle was demolished by a bomb in July 1973. Greencastle Catholic primary school was severely damaged. The Lido cinema, which had been purchased by the parish as the site for a new church, was severely damaged by fire. The Catholic population of this whole area was reduced to a fraction of its former strength.

When I visit Catholic parishes in west Belfast, I am constantly meeting people who were driven from their homes along the Shore Road or in east Belfast or north Belfast in those dreadful years following 1969. Memories of wrongs suffered in that recent past have undoubtedly played a role in the fostering of republican paramilitary violence. The IRA have at times been successful in exploiting these memories and in presenting themselves as defenders of Catholic communities against the danger of loyalist sectarian attack. Yet, I am constantly edified by the great lack of bitterness that I find among the immense majority of such people. I thank God for that spirit of forgiveness. It is one of the foremost marks of true Christianity.

EVIL OF LOYALIST MURDERS

There is a special quality of foulness about killing done for supposedly religious reasons. Sectarian murders have been a black stain across the pages of the history of this part of Ireland

81

over many generations, and the experience of recent years has sadly shown the resurgence in our society of sectarian violence.

All murders are deplorable, by whatever 'side' perpetrated, and they only serve to heighten tension and increase polarisation.

Loyalist murderers often claim to be acting in the name of the Protestant community. Their deeds are an insult to the Protestant name. They are a betrayal of the Protestant faith, which bases itself on the Word of God and which so strongly emphasises the sovereignty and the lordship of God. We sympathise with the Protestant community, in whose name such outrages claim to be perpetrated but whose members in their vast majority find such crimes abhorrent. We extend our admiration and our support to those Protestant clergy and laity who have had the Christian courage to denounce such deeds as an insult to the Protestant tradition.

For a Christian, murder is particularly heinous. Christ gave to those who follow him and bear his name a new commandment, the commandment to love one another. He said, 'By this all shall know that you are my disciples, by the love you have for one another' (John 13: 35). Christ commanded us to love our enemies, and by this to be recognisable as different from people who do not know Christ.

This divine commandment is not only a command given by God to the people He created; it is also a statement of the all-holiness of God and of His exclusive and sovereign lordship over life and death. In the Old Testament, the text of each Commandment is frequently followed by the words, 'I am the Lord your God' (see Exodus 20: 1; Deuteronomy 5: 6). It is because God alone is the Lord of life and death that men and women are solemnly commanded not to kill. Murder is a blasphemy against God as well as a crime against our neighbour.

UNIONIST PERCEPTION OF IRA CAMPAIGN

One of the many detestable consequences of the IRA campaign is the inevitable perception of it by the unionist community as a sectarian campaign waged against Protestants because of their religion. Virtually all members of the RUC, the RUC Reserve and the UDR killed by the IRA have been Protestants. Over recent years, nearly all those killed by the IRA have, in fact, been Protestants. The IRA claim that these persons are killed because they are members of the security forces and are therefore, in their odious terminology, 'legitimate targets'. From the unionist viewpoint, however, they have been killed or are listed as targets for killing because they are Protestants.

Many of these people have been shot when off duty, going quietly about their daily business or around their peaceful farms, or in their own homes, before their horrified wives or terror-stricken children. Many have been killed along border areas, where Protestants often live in isolated homesteads or communities. Protestants could not but see this murder campaign as a calculated policy to drive the Protestant population from these areas. Declaim as they may about their 'armed struggle against Crown forces', the IRA cannot shirk responsibility for this interpretation of their campaign as a nakedly sectarian one. Inevitably, all this heightens the fears, the tensions and the resentments of the Protestant community to danger point. In all this, I have not even spoken about the most infamous deeds of undisguised sectarian killings by members of the IRA or the INLA, notably the Whitecross and the Darkley massacres and the poorly disguised sectarian massacre at the cenotaph in Enniskillen on the occasion of a religious service on Remembrance Day.

ATTEMPTED MURDER OF GERRY ADAMS

The attempted murder in 1984 of Gerry Adams and his companions must be condemned as forthrightly and as unreservedly as any of the murder attempts and murders of the Troubles. It shares the same murderous mentality and is a manifestation of that evil spirit of hatred whom Our Lord challenged in His temptations: 'The Lord your God you shall adore and Him only shall you serve.'

St Patrick had to condemn violence among fellow Christians

in his time. He called it 'parricide, fratricide'. He wrote in his Letter to Coroticus: 'Let every God-fearing man know that they [the perpetrators] are enemies of me and of Christ, my God, for whom I am an ambassador.' He declared that such crimes were a destruction of the Law of God, which but recently God had excellently and kindly planted in Ireland.

## SECTARIANISM IN EMPLOYMENT

Discrimination in employment is still with us. After many years of admirable effort by the Fair Employment Agency, we still have a grossly unbalanced workforce, even, and perhaps particularly, in the industries that depend most heavily on government subsidy.

The recently enacted Fair Employment legislation appeared to be clear evidence of a government commitment to the elimination of existing inequalities. Before this was passed, I emphasised that for Fair Employment legislation to work it would have to be strong, effective, subject to mandatory monitoring and backed up by the necessary sanctions. It is depressing to see this long overdue package of basic civil rights being met with resistance by unionist politicians. It is even more depressing to note that it met with criticism and resistance from a few employers, who should instead have been leading the demand for equality of rights of access to work and for equality of rights and conditions in the workplace. It is indeed clear that without more employment there cannot be fair employment; it remains true that the two are inseparable. The implementation of the new legislation must place it beyond all doubt that inequalities in access to existing jobs will be removed over a reasonable time span, and that all new jobs will be fairly shared.

## PROTESTANT INSECURITY

The loyalist and Protestant community in Northern Ireland is marked by an extreme sense of suspicion, fear and insecurity. This is connected with the peculiar phenomenon of 'the double minority'. The Catholic population, a minority population in Northern Ireland, is a majority in the island of Ireland. The Protestant population, a majority in Northern Ireland, is a minority in the island of Ireland. Its traditions and experiences, both historically and even in the religious sphere, differ sufficiently from those of Protestants in Britain for it to be said that Northern Ireland Protestants are a minority in the British Isles as a whole. More and more they come to see themselves as a threatened minority, besieged and beleaguered, no longer able fully to trust Britain, distrusting the Republic of Ireland and fearing both the nationalism and, alas, the religion of its inhabitants; for some Ulster Protestants seem to make little distinction if any between peaceful and moderate nationalism on the one hand and terrorism on the other, or even between the IRA and the Catholic Church.

## CATHOLICS AND PROTESTANT RIGHTS

The importance of the Catholic Church's declaration to the New Ireland Forum about Protestant rights and freedoms has failed to secure the attention it merits. As the one chosen by the Irish bishops to lead their delegation to the New Ireland Forum, on 9 February 1984, speaking on behalf of the Catholic Bishops of Ireland, I said:

> The Catholic Church in Ireland totally rejects the concept of a confessional state. We have not sought and we do not seek a Catholic State for a Catholic people. We believe that the alliance of Church and State is harmful for the Church and harmful for the State. We rejoiced when that ambiguous formula regarding the special position of the Catholic Church was struck out of the Constitution by the electorate of the Republic. The Catholic Church in Ireland has no power and seeks no power except the power of the Gospel it preaches and the consciences and the conviction of those who freely accept that teaching . . .
>
> We are acutely conscious of the fear of the Northern Ireland Protestant community. We recognise their apprehensions that any political or constitutional or even demographic change in Northern Ireland would imperil their Protestant heritage . . . What we do here and now declare, and declare with emphasis,

is that we would raise our voices to resist any constitutional proposals which might infringe or might imperil the civil and religious rights and liberties cherished by northern Protestants. [*New Ireland Forum: Report of Proceedings*, Irish Episcopal Conference Delegation, p. 2]

## CHRISTIAN RESPONSE

The Inter-Church Working Party that produced the document *Violence in Ireland: a report to the Churches* in 1976, said, 'Ireland needs a programme to combat sectarianism, wherever it is to be found' (p. 72). The report declared:

> [The Churches] have not been vigorous enough or courageous enough in promoting social contacts and dialogue, especially at the level of ordinary people. Lack of contact, lack of dialogue, breed an environment of fear, suspicion, ignorance and prejudice, which can rightly be termed sectarian. It is to the elimination of this whole frame of mind that the combined efforts of the Churches need to be directed. [p. 72]

The report states:

> All organisations and bodies, not excluding the Churches themselves and certainly including those orders with religious or quasi-religious conditions of membership, must ask themselves fearlessly to what extent their actions and stances, no matter what their theological foundations, may contribute to the separation which can produce the terrible results that have occurred in recent years. [pp. 71–2]

The same report affirms:

> The most distinctive task confronting the Churches is to *promote and support reconciliation*. 'God ... has committed unto us the ministry of reconciliation.' The Churches must engage in the task of evangelism in a renewed effort to open men's hearts to the grace and truth of Christ. From this source can come forgiveness, patience, peace and reconciliation. Violence is an assault upon a brother made in the image of God and redeemed by Christ ... Reconciliation will mean acknowledging our own sins, being ready to forgive wrongs done against us and recognising that we have all, as individuals and institutions, things to

repent of – acts of omission, words ill-spoken and acquiescence in evil acts. We have not been the salt of the earth and the light of the world and have not expressed our faith in terms of social relationships. [p. 85]

Everyone in a position of leadership in the Churches, and indeed every Christian lay man and lay woman must do everything in his or her power, at whatever cost and in face of whatever opposition, to resist sectarianism and to try to eliminate it from our society. The greatest risk which we Churchmen could incur at the present time is the risk of not condemning and resisting evil; this would be tantamount to failing to confess Christ before men.

Christ gave us a special prayer that would be characteristic of his followers: we call it the Lord's Prayer. In it, we call upon God as '*Our* Father', thereby recognising that all who pray this prayer are brothers and sisters of one another, members of the one family. Sectarianism is a direct contradiction of that prayer. In that prayer we also link our forgiving of others with our plea to be ourselves forgiven by God. Implicitly, we are asking God not to forgive us if we are not ready to forgive those who have wronged us. Sectarianism or the desire for revenge are therefore implicitly asking God not to forgive us our own sins.

We must submit ourselves to the probing test of God's Word, which is

something alive and active; it cuts like any double-edged sword but more finely: it can slip through the place where the soul is divided from the spirit, or joints from the marrow; it can judge the secret emotions and thoughts. No created thing can hide from Him; everything is uncovered and open to the eyes of the One to whom we must give account of ourselves. [Hebrews 4: 12–13]

We must, in that light, recall St Paul's warning about 'grieving the Holy Spirit'. We must see it as a message specially addressed to all of us, Catholic and Protestant, and to all our Church communities, at this time of tension:

Do not use harmful words in talking. Use only helpful words, the kind that build up and provide what is needed so that what you say will do good to those who hear you. And do not make God's Holy Spirit sad; for the Spirit is God's mark of ownership on you, a guarantee that the Day will come when God will set you free. Get rid of all bitterness, passion and anger. No more shouting or insults. No more hateful feelings of any sort. Instead, be kind and tender-hearted to one another, and forgive one another, as God has forgiven you in Christ. [Ephesians 4: 29–32]

# 5
## PRISON POLICY:
## A KEY TO PEACE

*Bishops are called to be true fathers of all their people, excelling in the spirit of love and solicitude for all. They should have special care for those who live on the margin of society. Among those most needing pastoral care from Bishops are prisoners. My dear brothers, do not neglect to provide for their spiritual needs and to concern yourselves also about their material conditions and their families.*

*Try to bring prisoners such spiritual care and guidance as may help to turn them from the ways of violence and crime, and make their detention instead be an occasion of true conversion to Christ and personal experience of love. Have a special care for young offenders. So often their wayward lives are due to society's neglect more than to their own sinfulness. Detention should be especially for them a school of rehabilitation.* [Pope John Paul II, Address to the Irish Bishops in Dublin, 30 September 1979; in *The Pope in Ireland*, p. 63]

Since the late 1960s particularly, crime and punishment have become matters of major concern to the community in both parts of Ireland. They are topics for intensive, indeed passionate, public debate.

Much of the debate is, however, being conducted on the level of emotion and prejudice, not on the basis of reasoned argument and research. Elementary reactions of fear, frustration, anger, retaliation, revenge tend to predominate over rational discussion and empirical fact. Fundamental assumptions are not sufficiently questioned. Above all, there is little evidence, in Northern Ireland or in the Republic, that we have thought through our opinions of crime and punishment as a predominantly Christian community, or have tried hard enough to look at these problems from the standpoint of our Christian faith.

CHRIST AND THE PRISONER

When we turn to the Bible for light on the proper attitude to the prisoner, we find that prisoners are characteristically referred to as objects of divine pity, persons whom God promises to set free. The whole Exodus narrative turns on the concept of God's intervention in history to lead His people from captivity into freedom. 'To proclaim liberty to captives' (Isaiah 61: 1) is one of the prerogatives of the Messiah, one of the signs of the coming of the kingdom of God. A recurrent prayer in the Psalms is intercession on behalf of prisoners:

The Lord leaned down from His sanctuary on high.
He looked down from heaven to the earth
that He might hear the groans of the prisoners
and free those condemned to die.
[Psalm 101: 20–1]

It is [the Lord] who keeps faith for ever,
who is just to those who are oppressed.
It is the Lord who gives bread to the hungry,
the Lord who sets prisoners free.
[Psalm 145: 6–7]

A psalm which, the Gospels suggest, may have been prayed by Our Lord himself on the Cross, has these words:

The poor when they see it will be glad
and God-seeking hearts will revive;
for the Lord listens to the needy
and does not spurn His servants in their chains.
[Psalm 68: 33–4]

One of the models used in the Christian theology of redemption is the notion of a divine buying of the captive from enslavement, or deprivation of liberty, into emancipation. It is not just coincidental but deeply symbolic that, at the moment when Christ, the innocent, is condemned to prison to await execution, Barabbas, the guilty one, is released from jail.

Christ himself was once a prisoner. In the great Gospel scene depicting the Last Judgment, he identifies himself with prisoners: '[I was] in prison and you came to see me ... [I was] in prison and you never visited me' (Matthew 25: 35, 43).

In the precincts of the Church of St Peter in Gallicantu in Jerusalem, there is a dungeon in which, a certain tradition has it, Christ spent the night between his arrest and his crucifixion. The tradition holds that this church stands on the site of the house of Caiaphas. Whether the tradition is historically well founded or not is not so important. It does seem probable that the deep hole or well in the ground that pilgrims visit is similar to the type of dungeon in which Christ might have been confined. Many of the 'dungeons' referred to both in the Old Testament and in the New would seem to have been just such deep hollows in the clay, located in a king's or governor's palace or a military barracks, down into which the prisoner was lowered by ropes, and in which one was just able to stand but not recline, and from which there was no possibility of escape, since one could only be hauled up by ropes from above. Countless pilgrims have stood by that well-like dungeon in Jerusalem and have prayed Psalm 87, a psalm which might well have been prayed by Christ in prison, and which expresses so profoundly the feelings of so many prisoners throughout humanity's history:

Lord my God, I call for help by day;
I cry at night before you.
Let my prayer come into your presence.
Or turn your ear to my cry . . .

You have laid me in the depths of the tomb,
in places that are dark, in the depths.
Your anger weighs down upon me:
I am drowned beneath your waves.

You have taken away my friends
and made me hateful in their sight.
Imprisoned, I cannot escape;
my eyes are sunken with grief . . .

Wretched, close to death from my youth,
I have borne your trials; I am numb.
Your fury has swept down upon me;
Your terrors have utterly destroyed me.

They surround me all the day like a flood,
They assail me all together.
Friend and neighbour you have taken away:
My one companion is darkness.

Followers of Christ should, therefore, be characterised by compassion for prisoners, and even a certain fellow feeling for them. Christians should be conscious of being all of us liberated prisoners, set free through Christ's Passion, death and resurrection from captivity to sin into 'the glorious liberty of the children of God'. We should be conscious of being forgiven sinners, sinners in constant need of God's forgiveness, persistently recidivist and continually needing again to be pardoned and released. We cannot regard criminals and prisoners as outcasts, for we share the same condition. We need forgiveness just as much as they do; and we are taught by Christ that we cannot hope for forgiveness unless we are ourselves ready to forgive. Every time we repeat the Lord's Prayer, it has been said, we enter into a formal agreement or contract with God that we will forgive others if God will forgive us.

The fallen and sinful condition all men and women share is the basis for the Lord's prohibition of judgement. 'Judge not and you shall not be judged' (Matthew 7: 1). To judge others as if they were a distinct species of humans or sub-humans – guilty and sinful – in contrast to ourselves – who are guiltless and sinless – is to claim to be without sin. It is therefore equivalently to claim to be without need of forgiveness and redemption. It is ultimately to exclude ourselves from forgiveness and redemption. In the last analysis, it is to claim to be of another species than the humankind for whom Christ died. As St John says, it is to live a lie and exclude ourselves from the saving and liberating truth of Christ (1 John 1: 8–10). Gabriel Marcel used to say that the phrase 'Judge not and you shall not be judged' is the most fundamental statement of the metaphysics of man. It is certainly a fundamental statement of the Christian metaphysics of man.

Albert Camus, in his novel *La Chute*, presented the figure of the Judge-Penitent, the judge who cannot condemn because he is too conscious that he himself deserves condemnation. Camus suggests that in all human history there was only one brief moment when the true Christianity of unconditional forgiveness ever existed on this earth. It was during the three hours when Christ was hanging on the Cross, the victim of human injustice, cruelty and sin, yet judging no one, unconditionally forgiving everyone. This view is excessive. The ministry and the practice of forgiveness has always existed in the Christian Church. God's offer of reconciliation and forgiveness is at the heart of the Gospel of Christ. Nevertheless one can agree with Camus to the extent of admitting that much of the public attitude, and especially many of our own attitudes, to crime and criminals, to prisons and punishment, to offenders and prisoners, is a betrayal of true Christianity.

Awareness of our sinfulness, the sense of our need to turn to God for forgiveness, repentance and the desire to change our lives so that we may be ready to accept God's forgiving love and be reconciled to Him, accompanied by total trust in God's readiness to forgive, these are the basic elements in the Christian's response to God's self-revelation in Christ. God reveals Himself above all as the God of mercy and compassion, wishing not the death of the sinner, but desiring that he 'renounce his wicked ways and live' (Ezekiel 18: 23). Repentance, in its full original meaning of readiness for radical change of one's whole life and whole relationship with God, is inseparable from belief in Christ as Lord and Saviour. Christ began his public ministry by proclaiming, 'The time has come, and the kingdom of God is close at hand. Repent, and believe the Good News' (Mark 1: 15). Repentance and faith are inseparable. Consciousness of our sin, sorrow for sin and the desire to change our sinful ways, these are inseparable components of our faith in God, who in Jesus Christ shows Himself as a forgiving and saving God. St John puts it that recognising the truth about ourselves is a condition for accepting the truth which is God.

If we say we have no sin in us,
we are deceiving ourselves
and refusing to admit the truth;

but if we acknowledge our sins,
then God who is faithful and just
will forgive our sins and purify us
from everything that is wrong.
To say that we have never sinned
is to call God a liar
and to show that His word is not in us.
[1 John 1: 8–10]

Sinners constantly seeking to be reconciled with God and assured of His forgiveness, we Christians must in turn be ready
to forgive as we have been forgiven. We are asked by Our Lord
to 'love our enemies and pray for those who persecute us'
(Matthew 5: 44). We are called to forgive unconditionally and
without limit. We are to forgive our brother if he wrongs us
'not seven, but seventy times seven', that is to say, without any
limit (Matthew 18: 21–2). In other words a society will be truly
Christian in proportion to its readiness to forgive. It surely
follows that forgiveness, compassion, re-education and rehabilitation will be distinguishing characteristics of the prison system
in a Christian community, rather than merely punishment, ret-
ribution and deterrence.

## PRISONERS IN CHRISTIAN TRADITION

The Christian Church has never forgotten that she is summoned by her Master to a 'better way'. Prisoners have always
had a special place in the Church's mission of mercy. Imprisonment for the faith was a regular experience of the early
Christians, from the Apostles and St Paul onwards. St Paul
refers frequently to his prisoner's 'chains' and writes several of
his letters from a prison cell. Indeed imprisonment for the faith
is a recurring experience of Christians in every age. There may
well have been very many more Christians imprisoned or exiled
for their faith in this century than in any previous one.

Among the unforgettable experiences of the Synod of Bishops held in Rome in October 1990 was the presence among us,
for the first time, of bishops from Eastern Europe, many of

them recently released from prison after many years of penal servitude for their faith. One bishop from Romania recalled how ten of his fellow bishops had died in prison. The deeply moving testimonies of these contemporary confessors of their faith reminded us of the close links across the centuries between the Church and prisoners.

The visiting of prisoners was always held to be one of the Christian 'works of mercy'; it was sometimes called 'washing the feet of the saints'. St Justin Martyr, speaking about the celebration of the Eucharist, said:

> Those who are well-provided for, if they wish to do so, contribute what each thinks fit; this is collected and left with the President so that he can help the orphans and the widows and the sick, and all who are in need for any other reason, such as prisoners and visitors from abroad; in short he provides for all who are in want. [St Justin Martyr, *In Defence of the Christians*, chapter 67]

THE PRISON POPULATION IN IRELAND

The Church's apostolate of prayer and practical help for prisoners is more needed in Ireland today than ever. The prison population in both parts of Ireland increased dramatically during the past two decades. Subversive crime has been the greatest factor in this increase in Northern Ireland, where we now have the misfortune to have the highest proportion of prisoners to population in Western Europe, with a daily average of some 1,756 prisoners, or about 117 per 100,000 of the population. In the Republic of Ireland too the prison population has been increasing year by year over the same period at an alarming rate. In 1961, convicted prisoners numbered 1,731, and the daily average number of prisoners was 447. By 1982, the corresponding figures were a total of 2,557 convicted prisoners (an increase of 48 per cent) and a daily average number of 1,236 (an increase of 180 per cent). By the end of 1983, the daily average number of prisoners in the Republic went up a further 30 per cent to nearly 1,600. The continuance of paramilitary violence, the continuing increase in crime and the growingly strident calls for 'tougher' action against criminals all ensure that the prison population in both parts of Ireland will remain high. It is true that the Republic of Ireland has a proportionately smaller prison population than most European countries, with 55 prisoners per 100,000 population, as compared with the figure of 97 in England and Wales and 99 in Scotland. Sadly, however, the Republic of Ireland figure seems certain to go on rising.

Subversive prisoners are 4.2 per cent of the total prison population in the Republic of Ireland, with 18 per cent of those being from Northern Ireland. It is characteristic of subversive or politically motivated prisoners, both in Northern Ireland and in the Republic, that they are young, mostly in their twenties, that they have been convicted of serious offences, and that therefore they are serving long sentences, many of them life or indeterminate sentences. They regard themselves as prisoners of war, subject to an equivalent of military discipline, both from within and from outside the prison, and liable to cooperate with policy decisions or propaganda exercises determined by their organisations outside the prison. They accept it as an obligation and make it a point of honour to be constantly trying by every possible means to effect their escape. Consequently they pose a special security problem, and their presence tilts the balance of prison policy towards security rather than towards the other objectives of a humane prison system.

The characteristic methods, organisation and discipline of subversive groups are now being increasingly found also among professional criminals, who are a great and growing problem in society. They too have become highly efficient in their methods and tactics, inside and outside prison, they are supported by their own outside groups and are capable of ruthless reprisals against prison officers and other law-enforcement personnel and their families. The growth of professional criminal gangs and their increasing use of firearms constitute a new and grave problem for law-enforcement personnel and for prison authorities and prison officers.

The proportion of drug-users in prison populations is a

growing problem, especially in the Republic. In the last five years, that proportion has risen to some 40 per cent. Linked as it tragically is with the spread of HIV and the danger of AIDS within prisons, this is a new and very disturbing phenomenon. The implications for prisoners in general and for prison staffs can be quite frightening.

There is a steadily growing number of young prisoners. In the Republic of Ireland, nearly 80 per cent of all prisoners are between fifteen and thirty years of age, only some 10 per cent being between thirty and forty. The expectation seems to be that the number of young prisoners will increase rapidly over the coming years. It also seems to be taken for granted in our society that imprisonment is the most effective and perhaps the only way of eliminating crime. That assumption needs to be vigorously challenged.

## THE PRISON APOSTOLATE

The Church cannot remain indifferent, silent or inactive in respect of all these developments. She is called by her Master to have a special preference for the poor, and prisoners are a special category among the poor. First of all, deprivation of liberty is itself one of the most painful forms of deprivation, one of the most humiliating forms of dependency. Furthermore, the great majority of ordinary prisoners come from deprived sectors of society and from deprived neighbourhoods – the lower socio-economic groups, the unskilled or semi-skilled and lower-paid workers, the chronically unemployed, the undereducated, the school dropouts, the young people from broken homes or with alcoholic or violent parents. The Master has given us the Beatitudes not merely as guidelines for our discipleship, but as signs of what His kingdom is like. As Professor Joachim Jeremias says: the Beatitudes are 'examples of the kind of thing which happens when the Kingdom of God breaks through' (Prof. Joachim Jeremias, *Paroles de Jésus*, Les Éditions du Cerf, Paris, 1963, pp. 44–5). If the Church is credibly to proclaim the kingdom, she must aspire towards the blessing which Our Lord pronounced upon the poor. She must herself be poor in spirit, detached from the assumptions and the prejudices of the rich and the powerful, so as to be able to stand on the side of the poor. St Paul challenges us:

> Take yourselves at the time when you were called: how many of you were wise in the ordinary sense of the word, how many were influential people, or came from noble families? No, it was to shame the wise that God chose what is foolish by human reckoning, and to shame what is strong that He chose what is foolish by human reckoning; those whom the world thinks common and contemptible are the ones that God has chosen – those who are nothing at all to show up those who are everything.
> [1 Corinthians 1: 26–8]

> Treat everyone with equal kindness; never be condescending but make real friends with the poor. Do not allow yourself to become self-satisfied. Never repay evil with evil but let everyone see that you are interested only in the highest ideals. Do all you can to live at peace with everyone. Never try to get revenge.
> [Romans 12:16–19]

Our concern for prisoners is surely an important test of the degree to which we are living up to St Paul's precepts. The Church must try to educate the whole Christian community in its responsibilities towards prisoners, and indeed in respect of the penal and prison systems as a whole. One important way in which a community manifests the genuineness of its Christian faith is by its treatment of prisoners and its reaction to crime. Christians, with motivation derived from their faith, should be prominent among those who work professionally or voluntarily for the welfare of prisoners and ex-prisoners and for the welfare of their families. Church personnel and Church resources should be directed towards this area of Christian caring. Workers in the prison service or in related services, such as the probation service, prisoners' welfare services, boards of visitors, should find in this work an outstanding opportunity for expressing their faith in love. St Vincent de Paul began his great apostolate of charity by selling himself into captivity so that he could join the galley slaves who plied the boats for prosperous merchants between France and north Africa, in order to bring them to the faith of Christ and to show them the compassion of Christ. The Church's intercession has traditionally never neglected prayer for prisoners. This is part of the Solemn Intercessions in the Roman Liturgy of Good Friday. In the Roman Breviary in the period following Easter, one of the intercessions is: 'Through the exaltation of your Son raise up the sorrowful, set prisoners free, heal the sick – may the whole world rejoice in your wonderful gifts.'

The Church should not fail to remember prisoners and their families in her intercession, and to commend praying for prisoners to her members. The Church must ensure that the formation of candidates for the ministry and the ongoing education of the clergy should include insistence on the need for special pastoral care of prisoners and their families.

## SOCIETY'S MORAL AMBIVALENCE

The Church must also be concerned, in its preaching and catechesis, to correct the moral ambivalences reflected in our prison systems. For our prisons do mirror society's classifications of wrongdoing, crime and guilt. These classifications do not necessarily correspond with the Christian moral code.

Even a casual visitor to a typical prison will notice that the immense majority of the prison population come from the lower income groups, the more deprived parishes, the unskilled and semi-skilled sectors, the educationally deprived, the subliterate and subnumerate groups. Rarely does one find among prisoners persons from the middle or upper middle classes, professional people, moneyed people. Does this mean that there really is less crime among the rich than among the poor? Or does it mean instead that the rich have better chances of avoiding detection, or that they have a greater likelihood of a favourable outcome in court hearings because they are able to afford to pay better counsel or even perhaps because judges are more sympathetic to people who come from a background similar to their own? Outrage is likely to be aroused by even the faintest suggestion of bias in the judicial system. But there is in all of us a possibility of unconscious bias of background, upbringing, culture and class; and this bias is not inherently likely to be in most of us a natural bias in favour of the poor. The Irish Bishops' Pastoral, *The Work of Justice*, remarked in 1976 that a poor man's son has less likelihood of a lenient verdict in the courts than a rich man's son. At any rate, it must remain a puzzle for the social scientist and a challenge for the Christian that one seldom finds among prisoners persons convicted of insider dealings on the stock exchange, sharp practice in business takeovers, fraudulent diversion of industrial grants, tax frauds and tax evasion, clever manipulation of bankruptcy law. It is not either cynical or subversive to ask whether it is the real criminals who are in prison; or is it simply, in the words of Hemingway's *The Old Man and the Sea*, that 'the poor ain't never got no chance'.

## PRISON CHAPLAINS

The ministry of prison chaplains is now rightly being seen more and more as a specialised form of ministry, just as is hospital ministry. It is not always easy effectively to combine the work of prison chaplain with ordinary parish ministry. Particularly in the case of large prisons, and in view of our unusually large prison population and the predominance of youth in that population, a great deal of time and specific charisms and skills are needed if the chaplain is to establish relationships of trust with both prisoners and prison officers. The climate of prison tends to foster tension, mistrust and even resentment between prisoners and prison officers. The chaplain is committed to being a minister of reconciliation within the prison system; for this purpose it is vital that he merit the confidence, at one and the same time, of the prisoners and the prison authorities and staff. The chaplain cannot avoid having a certain pastoral responsibility towards the prison staff. This calls for exceptional qualities of prudence, patience, tact and integrity. The prison regime tends to engender a special psychology, both among officers and prisoners. Understanding of this psychology and coping with its consequences do not come easily to clergy whose commitment is limited in terms of time, availability and duration of appointment. Only full-time chaplains are, in many cases, able to meet the demands of the office.

The Church must take special care in the selection and training of prison chaplains. The chaplain should be assured of full support from his fellow clergy in parish ministry, and from the Church as a whole. In particular, the chaplain should be assured of the co-operation of the parish clergy in his work. He is, after all, caring for some of the most deprived and rejected members of parish communities. He has to show care for the families of prisoners, as well as for prisoners themselves. Indeed, the range of his caring is so wide that he should not be expected to carry the full burden alone.

THE FAMILIES OF PRISONERS

The impact of imprisonment on the community is not to be measured in terms of the numbers in prison alone. For each person incarcerated, there are many in the wider community who are affected by his fate. First and most obviously there is the immediate family, the spouse and children, the parents, the relatives and friends and neighbours, as the case may be the fiancé. In a society such as ours in Northern Ireland, with such a high proportion of prisoners, many of them young husbands and fathers, the impact of prison policy on community attitudes is very wide-reaching. At a rough guess, one could say that at least 10,000 people in Northern Ireland are affected by the imprisonment of a family member or relative. It is essential that government should pay continuous attention to this problem. It is vital that the Church be geared to meet this pastoral challenge. Pastoral care of prisoners' families must be seen as an important part of parish ministry. It must be remembered that imprisonment not only creates an enduring stigma for the prisoner himself, it also creates a stigma for the family of the prisoner, who, whatever the offence committed, must be presumed to be innocent sufferers.

As has been said, 'ordinary' (as distinct from paramilitary) prisoners very often come from deprived backgrounds. These people can be extremely sensitive. They can easily be led to suspect that the Church is more respectful of the middle classes, and shows less concern for and less interest in the poor and the marginalised. The Church, whose vocation is to be on the side of the poor, can easily come to be seen as the Church of the middle class and the privileged and powerful, the 'Establishment'. Pope Pius XI said that the great scandal of the nineteenth century was the loss by the Church of the working class. In Ireland, thank God, the Church retained the allegiance of the working class to a greater extent than in most Western countries. There is a real danger in our time that the Church in Ireland could lose the working classes. Pastoral concern for prisoners is one of the ways in which the Church can help to avert this danger. Neglect of prisoners and their families can certainly contribute towards the alienation from the Church of sections of the poor.

Pastoral care of prisoners must not be left to the clergy alone. The laity too must be involved. The whole Christian community must listen to the apostolic injunction, 'Do not forget the poor' (Galatians 2: 10). The provision of accommodation for discharged prisoners, assistance for them in reintegrating themselves into society, help in finding employment, these are some of the ways in which the Christian community must help.

IMPRISONMENT AND FAMILY LIFE

In 1983 the Holy See published a *Charter of the Rights of the Family*. This declares:

> The rights and necessities of the family, and especially the value of family unity, must be taken into consideration in penal legislation and policy, in such a way that a detainee remains in contact with his or her family and that the family is

adequately sustained during the period of detention. [Article
9(d), p. 13]

This is particularly relevant in our situation. In this light, one
must seriously question any policy which would systematically
deny 'open' visits to certain categories of prisoners. 'Closed'
visits permit no physical contact between a prisoner and his
wife and children. It is a painful deprivation for a husband not
to be able to embrace his wife or nurse his children. The experience can be traumatic for children, who cannot compre-
hend why they cannot sit on their father's knee. When the
prisoner is a woman, a wife, a mother, the problems are still
more acute. Very severe strain is caused for marriages by all
forms of prison regime; but the strain is greatly increased when
physical contact is forbidden, and when intimate conversation
is rendered impossible.

There are, undeniably, security risks, and security is one of
the legitimate concerns of prison authorities. Apart from the
real risk of the smuggling into prison of materials that might be
used by subversive prisoners for escape, there is for other prisoners the risk of the smuggling in of drugs. The authorities
should rightly expect co-operation from prisoners themselves
in the provision of open visits.

The stability of the family unit is also threatened when prisoners are detained in jails far away from their home, which
makes visits by spouses or children particularly difficult or pro-
hibitively expensive. The family is in general the strongest so-
cialising influence in a person's life. The family is normally the
greatest hope for the rehabilitation of the prisoner. Prison policy
should do everything possible to take cognisance of this fact.
For this reason, I urge that there should be a review of the
policy of transferring high-security prisoners frequently and
without warning from one prison to another. There have been
many instances of relatives undertaking the long, tiring and
expensive journey to Britain to visit a member of the family
only to find, when they arrive, that the prisoner has been trans-
ferred to another prison in a distant part of England. I believe
furthermore that without further delay there should be a review

of the policy of refusing transfer from English jails to prisons in Ireland, North or South, as the case may be, of prisoners who desire a transfer.

Another category of prisoners deserving special consideration are what are known as Secretary of State's Pleasure (SOSP) prisoners. These are usually prisoners whose offences were committed when they were very young, sometimes only minors, and who are detained indefinitely 'at the Secretary of State's pleasure'. When they have already served many years in jail, it is particularly demoralising for them and their families to have no idea how long their sentences will last and when a discharge can be expected. There have been indications recently of a more enlightened and compassionate attitude by government and prison authorities towards SOSPs and this is warmly to be welcomed. It is fervently to be hoped that policy will move even more rapidly in the direction of leniency towards these prisoners. After all, in nearly all cases, they have already served more than the equivalent of a life sentence as this is now computed in Britain and in many other countries.

Prisoners with indeterminate sentences should also have their cases reviewed regularly, so that, when possible, a date for their release should be determined without undue delay. It goes without saying, that in all these cases the security risks must be very carefully pondered, particularly where subversives are concerned, and moral certainty assured that the prisoner has severed his links with subversive organisations and is highly unlikely to become involved in subversive activity again. In Northern Ireland, it has to be said that the present mode of operation of the Life Sentence Review Board is in need of review. Inconsistencies have crept into the board's procedures. Favourable decisions that had all the appearances of precedents have been reversed in subsequent cases. Expectations have been aroused in the minds of prisoners, but have been bitterly dashed in the event.

The setting up of the Review Body was an enlightened measure. Paramilitary organisations opposed the measure and tried to dissuade their members from appearing before it.

Undoubtedly, they saw in it some threat to their own influence over prisoners. But in spite of this pressure, prisoners have increasingly been appearing before the Review Body. The Review Body was intended to bring hope into the lives of life sentence prisoners who hitherto had no human reasons for hope. This noble intention can be fulfilled only if the Review Body is always seen to operate fairly and on consistent criteria and to lead to an increasing number of determined dates for release.

In all these cases, serious attention must be paid to the impact on conjugal and family life of the interminable absence from home and family of long-sentence and especially life sentence prisoners. One of the great factors making for marital instability and the break-up of family life, and indeed the erosion of the social fabric, in many areas in Northern Ireland at the present time is imprisonment.

CLEMENCY

The British government and the Northern Ireland Office have in recent years begun to pursue a policy of greater compassion towards prisoners, and this is to be highly commended. Successive Secretaries of State and their Under-Secretaries have taken courageous decisions which included the closing of the Long Kesh compounds, the granting of compassionate parole to numbers of paramilitary prisoners at Christmas and more recently during the summer, and the speeding up of release dates and granting of more releases. Not one released life sentence prisoner or SOSP prisoner has become reinvolved in offence.

If it be argued that such decisions amount to 'going soft on crime or on terrorism', it must not be forgotten, least of all by Christians, that clemency has an important part to play in facilitating a change of heart, both in the offending individual and in the wider community. Authority has to make itself admired and not just feared; it has to make itself accepted and wanted and valued, not merely reluctantly obeyed. Authority and justice must be given a human face. Particularly when young people, who are at least in part victims of a violent society, become involved in crime, society cannot absolve itself from responsibility for the conditions that allowed or even encouraged them to be misguided. In the case of subversives, we are often dealing with people who 'in different circumstances . . . would be unlikely to run foul of the law', to quote the words of the study document *Punishment and Imprisonment* (p. 48) prepared by a joint working party of the Irish Catholic Commission for Justice and Peace and the Irish Council of Churches, and published in 1985. Some at least among them were idealistic young people who became caught up in the net of violence, their naive and youthful idealism having been exploited and manipulated for the perverse purposes and methods of an ideologically motivated cause. Prudent acts of clemency, conducted in a responsible and systematic manner, could be a recognition of society's collective responsibility for what the whole community did and failed to do in allowing a political and social situation to develop in which young people were left at the mercy of emotional and passional forces stronger than themselves.

I deal in a subsequent chapter with the case of a British Army private, Ian Thain, found guilty of the murder of a civilian allegedly mistaken for a paramilitary. In this case, it was claimed that this was a young man who had made 'a tragic error of judgement in very difficult circumstances'. One is by no means putting members of paramilitary organisations on the same footing as members of security forces when one points out that there are many young men, both loyalists and republicans, who similarly became victims of the tragic circumstances surrounding them in their early and middle teens and who made ruinous errors of judgement, with disastrous consequences for their young lives and often for their victims. Such young people are, at least in part, victims of a violent society. Society and in particular those responsible for political decisions in society cannot absolve themselves from their share of responsibility for the conditions that allowed or even encouraged these young people to be so calamitously misguided.

Our society is desperately in need of a change of heart. A change of heart cannot be forced, but it can be evoked. Only mercy can evoke mercy. Compassion cannot be compelled by force or fear; it can only be shown. By being shown, it justifies itself and indeed justifies justice. Clemency and mercy are not simply Christian virtues. They can also be forces for political change and social transformation. There are political and legal implications in St Paul's analysis of the decadent state of Roman society in his time. When he tells of men who have come to be 'without honour, love or pity', he speaks to our condition too. St Paul can find no escape from this 'body of death' except in 'the grace of God through Jesus Christ Our Lord' (Romans 7: 24). But let it be remembered that in Christian history 'grace' became a legal as well as a theological term. The grace of God given to us through Jesus Christ was held to call for answering human grace, even within the legal and the penal system. Hence the traditional concepts of 'the King's grace', 'the Queen's grace'. This legal concept had a biblical basis, as had so much else in the common law tradition. Even a society that often fell short of its Christian origins and inspiration could not forget St Paul's reminder that 'we have all sinned and fallen short of the glory of God' (Romans 3: 23) and can be justified only by 'the free gift of God's grace' (Romans 5: 17).

A prisoner in Rome composed a prayer on the occasion of a visit to the prison by Pope John Paul II that we could all make our own:

> Grant Lord . . . that the goodness coming from your heart may extinguish in us all anger, all bitterness, all hate, all intention of revenge, and may make us capable of suffering with humility for our own spiritual good. Give us back our dignity. Restore the bonds of love. Console all those dear to us. Hasten the day of our release. Prepare for all of us the day of eternal joy.

# 6
## PEACE THROUGH SOCIAL JUSTICE

*Since the purpose for which a political society is formed is the establishment of justice, the advancement of the common good and participation by all, that society will enjoy peace only to the extent that these three demands are respected. Peace can develop only where the elementary requirements of justice are safeguarded.*

*Unconditional and effective respect for each one's imprescriptible and inalienable rights is the necessary condition in order that peace may reign in a society . . . In a society in which these rights are not protected, the very idea of universality is dead, as soon as a small group of individuals set up for their own exclusive advantage a principle of discrimination whereby the rights and even the lives of others are made dependent on the whim of the stronger. Such a society cannot be at peace with itself: it has within it a principle leading to division . . . To the extent that the rulers of a particular country apply themselves to building a fully just society, they are already contributing decisively to building an authentic, firmly based and lasting peace.* [Pope John Paul II, Message for World Day of Peace, 1 January 1982]

SOCIAL INJUSTICE

There are many injustices in our society, and there can be no lasting peace or stability until these injustices are tackled. A fundamental injustice of our time is massive unemployment and the unfair distribution of resources, job opportunities, housing conditions and educational opportunities among the haves and the have-nots in the community.

For the undeniable evidence that social and economic conditions play a major contributory part in the continuing violence, I invite those interested to procure shaded maps of Belfast and of Northern Ireland showing degrees of intensity of paramilitary operations, and then compare them with maps illustrating percentages of unemployment, extent of deprivation and poverty,

113

and degrees of dependence on social welfare and supplementary benefits. The closeness of correlation is immediately obvious.

I wish to speak about people's human rights, their dignity as persons, their right not to be denied the opportunity to fulfil their full potential as human beings and as Christians. I wish to speak about these things in the context of deprived and economically undeveloped regions such as west and north Belfast, an area of vast public neglect, where many thousands of people are denied these opportunities. I speak primarily of Catholic west and north Belfast and, as I am using the term here, this extends from the lower Falls Road out to Poleglass and from Divis Flats to Ardoyne and Ligoniel. But I wish to state that the same picture is to be found in adjacent areas of Catholic east Belfast such as Ballymacarrett and the Short Strand, as well as in the Markets and lower Ormeau Road. I wish to state also that the same situations are to be found in the Shankill Road and in Protestant working-class areas in north Belfast and elsewhere.

If one were to visit homes in the Shankill and listen to people's real problems and needs, one would not find them basically different from those that one finds along the Falls. In both communities, one will meet the same recurring preoccupations, namely jobs and job opportunities, schools and careers for children, the cost of living, the payment of bills and arrears, the desire for an end to the Troubles, the longing for peace.

UNEMPLOYMENT

Unemployment is one of the great social evils and injustices of our time, and is the source of multiple personal, familial and community sicknesses. West Belfast has some of the highest unemployment figures to be found anywhere in Western Europe. The Northern Ireland Housing Executive Greater Belfast Household Survey of 1985 showed an unemployment rate of 47 per cent in inner west Belfast and 37.6 per cent in outer west Belfast. Current official figures from the live register for the different electoral districts, when translated into percentages of the economically active population, show male unemployment rates of more than 50 per cent in several districts.

The official figures manifestly fall short of the real unemployment rates. Female unemployment figures show only those women who claim unemployment benefit. The figures for workers on Action for Community Employment (ACE) schemes are in effect little more than deferred unemployment figures, since the vast majority return to unemployment at the end of their twelve-month ACE work experience. In west Belfast, possibly at least three-quarters of Youth Training Programme (YTP) trainees are being trained for jobs that do not exist and types of job that are never likely to exist. The ACE and YTP schemes are most certainly welcome and the situation would be very much worse without them. But they are no substitute for government initiatives to create real jobs.

Unofficial but reliable local surveys in a number of west Belfast parishes indicate unemployment rates of upwards of 60 per cent and in one or two cases as high as 80 per cent of the working population. Of the 13,000 to 15,000 unemployed persons in Catholic west Belfast, more than half have been unemployed for more than a year.

In Ballymurphy, a typical area of west Belfast, even in the days of relatively full employment in Northern Ireland unemployment never at any time fell below 30 per cent. In the early days of the 1960s, when unemployment in Lisburn stood at about 5 per cent, when unemployment in Antrim also stood at about 5 per cent, the unemployment rate in Ballymurphy was 35 per cent. Unemployment in the area is reckoned to stand now at well over 65 per cent. To put this in perspective, we can compare this figure with that from unemployment blackspots in Britain that were in the news some years ago as a result of rioting, such as the boroughs of Lambeth and Brixton. Unemployment in Lambeth stands at 22 per cent, in Brixton at 33 per cent. These are universally regarded as disaster areas. Unemployment in Ballymurphy, however, I repeat, stands at 65 per cent. But Ballymurphy and many other similar Catholic areas in Belfast are largely forgotten about. Reports about them usually concentrate on symptoms, such as violence, car-stealing, vandalism. Rarely is any analysis attempted of the underlying causes of these symptoms, namely massive unemployment and social deprivation. Still more rarely is media attention given to the tremendous fortitude, cheerfulness and generosity of the people who live there but refuse to let their spirit be crushed by the adversities that beset them.

West and north Belfast are fast becoming a great pool of de-skilled labour. Unemployment is becoming self-perpetuating. Lack of previous skilled work experience is a disqualification for west Belfast people when they apply for industrial jobs. They are caught in an unemployment trap.

Recent social welfare changes and cuts are claimed, among other things, to provide incentives for people to go out and find jobs instead of remaining 'on the dole'. The cruel irony is that the cuts hit hardest in areas like west and north Belfast, where for the majority there are no jobs to be found.

Those with jobs are a privileged minority. Often they are those whom society has favoured and subsidised, giving them better education and better opportunities. In modern society, it is very largely a myth that people succeed primarily because of their superior entrepreneurial spirit, their self-drive and self-reliance. Such qualities are undeniably an element in business and professional success. But they must not lead us to ignore the immense contribution made by the taxpayer, namely by society as a whole, to every business or professional success story. Every industrial enterprise now benefits from massive public subsidy, both in terms of direct grant and in terms of tax relief and tax incentive. Every industrial worker is a beneficiary of state subsidy. Every new industrial job is subsidised. It is paradoxical that industrial grants are regarded as rewards for enterprise, while unemployment benefits are regarded as dole money for the work-shy or for 'welfare spongers'.

Disparaging remarks about the unemployed as 'being better off idle than working' are almost always untrue, unjustified and injurious. Very few persons choose or prefer to be unemployed.

Only in rare cases and for short periods is anyone better off unemployed than working. Unemployment and welfare benefits are no proper substitute for wages. Even an enlightened welfare society is saying to people, 'We will pay you just enough to live on, but we do not really need you. Society can function very well without you. Indeed you are a burden on society.'

This is demoralising. It is destructive of a person's self-esteem. Unemployment is a cause of tension in marriages and of dissension in families. For the young, a job is a symbol of independence. To have a job is to be an adult, to begin to have one's own earned money and to have some control over one's own life. Not to have a job and never to see hope of a job is to be drawn close to hopelessness. It feeds the spirit of resentment and rebellion.

Although there are no Protestant areas remotely as badly off in terms of unemployment as are west Belfast and other Catholic areas in Belfast and throughout the North, nevertheless there is heavy unemployment in the Protestant communities also, particularly in urban working-class areas like those I have mentioned. There are glaring differences in living standards between the social classes, and these differences are widening, not lessening, with the years.

SOCIAL CLASS DIVISIONS

In Northern Ireland, the membership of political parties and the polarisation between them, and even the problems of political conflict, are aggravated and the difficulties of finding solutions are compounded by the polarisation between social classes, not only across the two communities but within the Catholic and the Protestant communities respectively. A great gulf is fixed between middle-class Protestants and working-class Protestants, between middle-class and professional Catholics and working-class or unemployed Catholics. Political options and electoral practices are to a considerable extent influenced by these class divisions, and by the spatial segregation that accompanies them. The grip of paramilitary organisations on communities, the

117

political cover accorded to paramilitary groups, and the electoral support given to political organisations supporting paramilitary organisations exist largely in urban working-class areas and in rural small-farming communities. Political organisations such as Sinn Féin derive much of their appeal from their credibility in presenting themselves as a party of the working class and small farmers, identified with the idiom, mentality, community psychology, experience and self-image, grievances, resentments and hurt of the working class (and for 'working class' one should often read 'unemployed class'), and from their immense skill and, in important measure, their sincerity in committing themselves to remove the grievances of that under-class and liberate them 'once and for all' from the oppression and injustice that has marked and continues to mark their lives.

Much the same could be said of the Democratic Unionist Party (DUP). Each cleverly and successfully cultivates, channels and exploits the grievances of the working class and small-farmer sectors of the population and mimics their resentments and suspicions of the middle-class 'Establishment', the 'Establishment political parties' and even the 'Establishment Church'. Each creates its hate figures, whether it be 'the Brits' or the 'Brit-lovers' on the one hand or the 'republicans', the 'Romanists' or the 'ecumenical clergy' on the other. The politics of each of these opposing groups could fairly be described as the politics of resentment or the politics of anger.

These aspects of political conflict in our society have not received anything like the attention they deserve. The correlation of political conflict with class differences and with socio-economic factors needs to be given much more attention, whether in the inner city or in the newer estates. The Churches must work tirelessly to bridge the gap of incomprehension between their own middle-class and working-class communities and to make their more prosperous members conscious of the real injustice and deprivation suffered by working-class and unemployed groups and of their own responsibility towards the disadvantaged within their own household of faith. Attention has frequently been called to the opting-out of the middle classes from political and social responsibility. It is undoubtedly true that our present political polarisation and stagnation are facilitated by this opting-out on the part of the more educated and articulate people in society, who ought to be putting their intelligence, their education, their experience and their skills at the service of the total community and specifically of the less advantaged groups.

Class segregation is greatly compounded in our situation by the increasing physical segregation between the Protestant and the Catholic communities, whether middle-class or working-class. Recent studies of housing policy lead to the depressing conclusion that denominational segregation in housing is not merely something that has been happening at an increasing rate over the past two decades as a result of voluntary decisions by individuals and families. It is not just the continuing consequence of the massive enforced movements of population through sectarian rioting and intimidation in the 1970s. It is also due to policy decisions made by the Housing Executive, which operates under the overall policy directives laid down by the Department of the Environment. In other words, it is a result of government policy. This sad but well-substantiated conclusion is reinforced by observation of the solid and permanent dividing walls that continue to be built between denominational enclaves, and the wide motorways and link roads carefully situated in such a way as to divide Catholic from Protestant areas, in addition to other depressing signs that denominational segregation is being institutionalised as a permanent phenomenon of life in Northern Ireland.

Sad though it be to admit it, this physical segregation may have contributed to the decline in sectarian rioting and intimidation in working-class residential areas that were such a tragic feature of our urban history in the early 1970s. In the short term, planners might feel justified in accepting segregation in the interests of inter-community conflict-free coexistence. Surely, however, this short-term gain, if such it be, is outweighed by the longer-term obstacles to political normalisation and a genuinely reconciled society in the future which are thereby created.

In too many circles there is a perception that the troubles of west Belfast are self-inflicted. This perception is grossly unfair and unjust. It is true that west Belfast is one of the principal theatres of IRA violence directed against the security forces but also against civilians, including employers and workers, whom the IRA choose to identify as collaborating with the British authorities. The IRA also operate various forms of extortion and intimidation, affecting businesses, traders, building contractors. IRA attacks on the security forces make ordinary policing extremely dangerous and difficult; this in turn leads to a serious breakdown of law enforcement and a disastrous increase in attacks against the person and property and in all forms of lawlessness. All this creates a climate extremely unattractive to potential investors and unfavourable for industrial development.

Any hope or sign of improvement in the economic environment in areas like west or north or central Belfast are clearly seen by the IRA as a danger to their campaign. Any promise of improved job prospects is seen by them as a threat. Improvement and reform are anathema to the dedicated revolutionaries they are. Improvement and reform must be resisted and wrecked, because they imperil the revolutionary struggle. The existing order must be destroyed before the revolutionary utopia can be built. This is why factories or small enterprise centres like the former Midland Hotel must be bombed. This is why normality and jobs in city centre Belfast must be wrecked. This is why Castle Court in central Belfast must be targeted. This is why job hopes for west and north Belfast must be sabotaged.

The deterioration in the quality of life in west Belfast is certainly in part a consequence of the IRA's campaign. Indeed it is not simply an indirect and unintended consequence. It would seem to be actually part of the IRA's revolutionary strategy. The ideology of revolution, which the IRA share, is that the conditions of life of an oppressed people must worsen to a point where the sufferings become unbearable, for only then will people see that nothing but total revolution will bring change and justice. If the conditions of life are not worsening of themselves, the revolutionary movement will act to make them worse and thereby hasten 'our day', the day of revolution. Economic decline, social deprivation, the breakdown of law and order become elements in the strategy of revolution; efforts to improve the situation through constitutional and peaceful methods are seen as 'reformist', 'counter-revolutionary' and 'reactionary' activities which must and will be resisted and wrecked. 'Reform' becomes a bad word, and those who advocate reforms are condemned as 'Establishment people', 'reformists', 'collaborators' and 'enemies of the revolution'.

Let no one pin the blame nor the shame of breakdown of law and order on the Catholic people at large in these areas. They are its victims, not its authors. They are its sufferers, not its perpetrators. The people of these areas are a great people, resilient, brave, cheerful in adversity, dignified in sorrow, with qualities of neighbourliness, hospitality and generosity that deserve admiration. A grievous wrong is done to them by those who through their brutal behaviour give a bad and a false image to their areas. Those who behave lawlessly are few. Those who incite them to lawless behaviour are fewer still. Let no one blame the whole community for the misdeeds of a small and unrepresentative fraction.

GOVERNMENT COMMITMENT

Such success as the IRA has had in winning and sustaining active or passive support in deprived areas has been facilitated and in part caused by the lack of positive and co-ordinated government policy in respect of sectors like west and north Belfast. Government has been determined not to allow west Belfast to become a no-go area in respect of security. The great majority of west Belfast people welcome this determination and have no desire to be left to the mercy of the IRA. But there

121

must be an equal determination on the part of government not to allow west Belfast to become a *de facto* no-go area in respect of industrial investment, infrastructural redevelopment, urban renewal, and public services and amenities generally.

West Belfast has not chosen to become a ghetto. Its great concentration of Catholic people is the result in large part of official government housing policy under the old Stormont regime. West Belfast's Catholic population has been swollen over many decades by the influx of Catholics driven out of mixed areas elsewhere in Belfast by organised sectarian intimidation by loyalist gangs. Such intimidation has recurred at twenty-year intervals over more than a century, and very notably in the 1970s. West Belfast has become ghettoised by society and by a long absence of concerted government planning, as much as by IRA violence. It is time to expose and refute the claim that some kinds of public facility must be located only in places that are 'accessible to both communities', and therefore not in west Belfast. The people of west Belfast are citizens with the same rights as citizens anywhere. Public facilities should be located on grounds of need and population density, not on grounds of the political or other complexion of the population.

INDUSTRIAL DEVELOPMENT BOARD

On the industrial scene, there was good reason to believe that the Industrial Development Board (IDB) had for many years virtually written off west Belfast. Apart from the ill-starred De Lorean venture and Strathern Audio, no other major industrial project had been attracted to west Belfast in twenty years until the timely and welcome arrival of Montupet in 1989. Meanwhile, factory after factory has closed down. Mackie's, the only substantial industrial employer left, is moving out. Abandoned factories have been allowed to deteriorate to a state that would discourage potential clients rather than attract them. The American Monitor plant might have been put on the market by the IDB but for the initiative of a community group of professional and business people giving of their time and talent voluntarily to try to create small enterprise units. The IDB will

122

claim factory developments along Boucher Road and elsewhere as evidence of its commitment to west Belfast. People who know the area will quickly point to the contrast between Boucher Road and the other side of the motorway, and will ask how much the Catholic part of west Belfast will benefit from the Boucher Road developments – however much one rejoices to see jobs being provided for anyone at this time of economic recession.

## DIVIS FLATS

Unemployment is not the only kind of social and economic suffering endured in west Belfast and similar areas. Multiple sufferings are inflicted on the people of such areas by the conditions in which they are obliged to live.

Let me speak about conditions in the Divis Flats complex. After a week spent visiting the Flats in March 1985, I said in St Peter's Pro-Cathedral:

> Following my visit of the Complex, I have to say quite categorically that, in my opinion, there is no acceptable solution to the problems of the Divis Complex other than complete demolition of the flat-blocks and their replacement by conventional housing.

During October 1985, I visited many flats in the complex again and I had to repeat, with even greater emphasis, what I had said the previous March. It was my firm conviction that no refurbishing would ever make Divis an acceptable human environment. I suggest that anyone who tours the flats and sees the conditions and talks to the people who live there could come to no other conclusion. Cosmetic exercises such as external painting might give the impression to passing motorists on the Westlink or the Falls Road that the flats are a pleasant and even attractive complex; but they merely cover over internal conditions quite unworthy of human dignity.

The flats had fundamental design faults and structural flaws from the very beginning, and these have become more glaring with the passage of time. Heating was a problem from the start. Problems with plumbing, dampness and condensation, insect infestation and refuse disposal have recurred endlessly. A dangerous amount of asbestos is used in the panelling. Fire precautions are seriously deficient. The worst feature of the flats has been their total unsuitability as family dwellings. It is incredible that proper drying facilities for wet clothes were never installed. Until the introduction of launderette facilities a few years ago by Cathedral Community Services, clothes had to be dried on radiators or hung out on window balconies or suspended from clotheslines in bathrooms. One can imagine the problems arising for mothers with small children.

Outside the complex, few could believe that there is no provision for play spaces for children – even if parents could risk allowing their children to go downstairs and out of their sight in order to play. For most of the day, mothers are literally imprisoned with their children in the flats. When they must go out for necessary errands the difficulties they face are simply intolerable. Much more often than not, the lifts, mean as they are, do not work. Mothers have to carry prams and babies down flight after flight of stairs, and then carry them up again, further burdened with shopping bags. In the flats one can meet mothers with very small children, who have to carry a pram down seven flights of stairs and leave it at the bottom, then climb up again for one baby, descend and strap it into the pram on the ground floor, and then climb again up all those weary flights of stairs to bring down the other toddler, before going on their errands; and then repeat the whole exercise on returning. The narrow steps of the stairways, often dangerously chipped and broken, are a real hazard, complicated by the fact that the stairways are often unlit. High-rise complexes like Divis are totally unsuited for families with children.

The Divis Flats are rendered still more unsuitable for families by the practice, which seems to be increasing, of renting out vacant flats to families or individuals whose behaviour is antisocial and constitutes a disturbance, if not a real danger, to their neighbours. Old people are often afraid to go outdoors at all, and are virtually confined to their flats for weeks on end. If the situation continues to be neglected and a solution is postponed indefinitely, the area will deteriorate still further into a slum of nineteenth-century proportions.

Let no one say that the people who live there have brought the problems on themselves. Certainly there are vandals, 'hoods', joyriders, drinkers, glue-sniffers. But these phenomena are, in a very significant degree, the consequences and not the causes of bad housing conditions and a degrading environment. There is furthermore the pernicious paramilitary presence, which imposes new forms of oppression on an already oppressed people. There is consequent constant harassment of innocent residents by security force patrols and searches. But let it be firmly stated and let it be recognised by all that the people of Divis and of the lower Falls in general are a wonderful people, whose spirit a bitter history and a harsh present have been unable to break. They do not deserve the environment into which past planning blunders and continuing social neglect have locked them. They do not deserve the stigma that middle-class society often attaches to them. Society owes the people of Divis a chance, and then they will be seen for what they truly are, a warm and welcoming and caring community. Indeed it is a tribute to their great human and community qualities that the people of Divis have retained their dignity and self-respect and their basic law-abiding and peace-loving values in spite of conditions as bad as those which have at times turned some areas in Britain into rioting battlegrounds.

The announcement by the Northern Ireland Housing Executive of its intention to demolish the Divis Flats complex and replace it by conventional housing was the best news the lower Falls heard in a long time. But progress is painfully slow. It is fervently to be hoped that cutbacks in the housing budget will not be allowed to drag out the Divis demolition and re-building programme still further.

What I have said about Divis Flats can equally be said about Unity Flats and other high-rise complexes in north Belfast.

WORK OF THE HOUSING EXECUTIVE

The new replacement housing being provided by the Housing Executive in Divis and elsewhere is of superb quality and could serve as a model for urban housing redevelopment anywhere. The best of the new public sector housing being provided by the Housing Executive is scarcely to be bettered in any other city in Ireland or Britain. This is an essential part of the only effective policy for the eventual ending of violence. The Kerner Commission, which reported on city riots in the USA in the late 1960s, said:

> The only genuine, long-range solution for what has happened lies in an attack – mounted at every level – upon the conditions that breed despair and violence. All of us know what these conditions are: ignorance, discrimination, slums, poverty, disease, not enough jobs ... Something imaginative and dramatic is needed, both to prevent the waste of public monies and to create a new sense of hope and patience in the communities.

In the policies and practice of the Housing Executive, Northern Ireland offers to the world a model of political impartiality in respect of allocation of housing, as well as a model of quality and standards in publicly owned housing. Our shortcomings in the matter of housing – and they are still many and serious – lie in the area of the overall housing budget rather than in the area of fair distribution of that budget.

INFRASTRUCTURAL REDEVELOPMENT

West Belfast has been allowed to take on all the appearances of urban blight and industrial wasteland. It has fallen behind almost all comparable areas in terms of arterial roads and approach roads, road frontages, shopfront refurbishment and general environmental renewal. This environmental neglect serves as a deterrent to potential industrial investors and is depressing and demoralising for the inhabitants. The people of west Belfast deserve better.

While saying this, I have also to record my gratitude for the commitment of government departments and their officials and agencies to generous aid for many employment and community services schemes in west Belfast parishes. I have regretfully to add that these schemes and Church involvement in them have come under criticism from some who profess a commitment to justice for oppressed people in west Belfast. The Church and the clergy are accused of being 'agents of British counter-insurgency' policy, and of virtually controlling British government funding allocation to west Belfast, but at the cost of being controlled by British government interests.

The accusations are preposterous and they are false. They stand self-condemned by the distortions and plain untruths used to buttress them. They are harmful to the real interests and job hopes of the people. These accusations cast a slur on clergy who are working so hard and so effectively to defend a community's rights to jobs, dignity and social justice. They constitute a slander on scores of dedicated lay people who are giving voluntarily of their time, their business experience and their professional skills, without any personal benefit or gain or profit, to promote the economic regeneration and improve the quality of life of communities long neglected by state, city council and public. Any government grant allocations are long overdue and hard-fought. The projects that have been grant-aided have been carefully researched by volunteer professionals and meet all the exacting criteria laid down by statutory agencies.

Let it not be forgotten that government grants to west Belfast are not concessions; they are not handouts. The people of west Belfast, like citizens and taxpayers everywhere, are entitled as of right to their full share of all public expenditure. They have been neglected too long. The clergy and lay people who have worked for them and with them to secure their rights deserve praise and admiration, not criticism. They do not make speeches or organise marches. They deliver jobs, and this is a work of justice and thus an integral part of evangelisation. These clergy and lay people are doing in Irish conditions what bishops, priests, religious and lay people are rightly praised for for doing in Latin America. The community projects of Catholic parishes throughout west, north and east Belfast can be called examples of authentic, applied liberation theology.

FINDING A WAY FORWARD

But all these programmes, however welcome and encouraging,

127

are inadequate to tackle the basic underlying problem of chronic unemployment. All the elements of the west Belfast problem are interlinked and interdependent. A comprehensive and integrated plan of overall redevelopment is needed. The chief responsibility for devising and researching this plan and for implementing it must rest with government. Local groups from the community, with the necessary business experience and skills, will certainly help. The dedication and commitment of some of these groups are beyond praise and they offer a precious resource to government. But they cannot discharge the goverment's responsibilities for it. All efforts at socio-economic rehabilitation of west Belfast will fail unless there is firm political will, a comprehensive phased plan, and a large commitment of public funds.

All government departments and agencies must be involved. But it is not enough that each government and civil service department make its contribution in isolation. A co-ordinated interdepartmental approach is imperative, with competent and authoritative overall supervision and direction.

One unfortunate fact is that there are so few people at any decision-making level of the civil service who have personal knowledge of the west Belfast area or sufficient understanding of and empathy with the west Belfast community. Serious efforts must be made to identify and recruit into the civil service talented people with this kind of understanding and empathy.

There are plenty of examples of multi-factor urban redevelopment available in Britain, the Republic of Ireland and in Europe, that can stimulate thinking as to what is needed in west Belfast. Many agencies and initiatives already exist in Northern Ireland that can make powerful contributions to the overall plan. But they need to be extended and they need to be co-ordinated.

Part of the modern concept of urban renewal is that private sector investment should be attracted to top up government grants. Attracting private sector interest in west Belfast will not be easy, at least in the initial stages, although it is hoped that the Confederation of British Industry (CBI) will strongly support such efforts. The International Fund for Ireland could take the place of the missing private sector investment and top up government funding in the west Belfast redevelopment plan. Few claims upon that fund are more clearly in line with its aims of community reconciliation than the deghettoisation of greater west Belfast.

It must be clearly seen, however, that International Fund for Ireland money is additional to and not an alternative for government funding. It must also be seen that the new government funding for west and north Belfast is additional to the funding already available from existing sources like LEDU, the small business agency for Northern Ireland, and also that it is not siphoned off into routine activities for which public funding is already statutorily available.

A radical new approach is needed to industrial training in west Belfast. The emphasis should shift from low-quality training to the high-quality training relevant to the kind of jobs that will be available in the technological industrial revolution of the present and the future. An information technology workshop should be located in west Belfast similar to the Quest I-Tech Workshop in Linenhall Street, under the auspices of the Department of Economic Development. The Quest I-Tech Workshop is reckoned to have a 70–75 per cent employment success rate, compared with an employment rate, in real job terms, that may be as low as 12–15 per cent for west Belfast YTP schemes.

We now have new and unique opportunities in west and north Belfast to develop educational curricula related to the real community situation and geared to identified needs. The management team of the new Corpus Christi College, catering primarily for boys of the middle and lower Falls, is planning imaginative new curricular developments that will be relevant to any new development plan for west Belfast. The work of St Louise's Comprehensive College in the same Falls Road area is already widely known and rightly praised.

The further education facility recently established in the former St Thomas's secondary school, now the Whiterock

Centre, is offering exciting new training and community education possibilities, with programmes closely related to local community needs and to the overall and long-term needs of greater west Belfast. One fascinating new development in further education is the concept of 'open learning', as developed in the Open College In-house Centre. This has interesting possibilities on the Whiterock site. Indeed the educational facilities at every level in west Belfast are motivated and eager to make their full contribution to that essential infrastructure of all economic and community development that is education.

We have unrivalled research resources to hand in Queen's University and the University of Ulster. These great institutions can find a magnificent opportunity for innovative thinking in applying their skills to the socio-economic redevelopment of west and north Belfast and to researching new products with development potential for such areas. They have already done much and extremely valuable work in analysing the problems – political, social, socio-psychological and economic – of west and north Belfast. They have an important contribution to make now in researching solutions.

It is time for a new deal in west and north Belfast. From being a problem and an embarrassment, these areas must be seen now as a challenge and an opportunity. A concerted redevelopment plan for west and north Belfast will do far more for the ending of violence than any security policy, important though this be. Government must lead the way in demonstrating that there is a peaceful way to justice, and that it works. Government must press resolutely on with a comprehensive redevelopment programme for west and north Belfast. In particular, this programme needs a much greater commitment of money, resources and specialist manpower than it has yet received. Money spent on this will bring greater and more lasting returns than increased security budgets.

The Making Belfast Work initiative, launched by Tom King as Secretary of State in July 1988 and enthusiastically continued by his successor, Peter Brooke, and their respective ministers, has the potential to make a significant contribution towards achieving the objectives outlined above. After two decades of decay and neglect, the initiative has been slow to get airborne and there is still not enough evidence of a coherent and comprehensive plan, an integrated strategy and an adequate allocation of resources. We must, however, gratefully acknowledge the commitment of the NIO and the head of the Northern Ireland Civil Service, Sir Ken Bloomfield, as well as that of the many dedicated people working in the statutory and voluntary agencies, the Belfast Action Team workers and the voluntary development boards who are collaborating in the overall effort. All concerned should take heart from the results already achieved and be convinced that this is indeed the way to a peaceful, prospering and gradually reconciled Belfast.

The new Springvale development announced in 1990 by Richard Needham, Minister for Economic Development, which is planned to span Catholic and Protestant sectors in west and north Belfast, promises to be an important element in an overall redevelopment programme, and at the same time a major factor for reconciliation of divided communities.

THE ROLE OF THE CATHOLIC COMMUNITY

The Catholic community in west and north Belfast has a vital role to play in any rehabilitation plan for the area. Government can count on great public welcome and full community support for any comprehensive plans they bring forward for the redevelopment of these areas. The community will play its part in working to make the area a source of pride to residents and visitors, and to create in it an environment worthy of its great people.

Local priests and many men and women in the local communities, and many people with business or professional skills who are residents or natives of the parishes, are working and will continue to work tirelessly to promote job creation, attract industrial investment, foster small business and service enterprises, and establish job training oriented towards real jobs, especially in advanced technology.

Communities at street and parish level must be concerned about improving the environment, doing all they can to discourage graffiti writing and to clean up graffiti, in general, keeping their neighbourhood a place of which they and visitors can be proud.

Parents must do all they can to keep their children away from vandalism and from contact with paramilitaries. The many parents who do succeed in this task deserve the highest praise. Parents must support the work of their children's teachers, in respect of both the religious and the secular programmes of the schools.

The Catholic community in the rest of the city and the diocese, especially in the more advantaged parishes, will also lend their support and help. In the spirit of the early Church, as described in the Acts of the Apostles which we read in the Eastertide liturgy, we shall try to share the gifts God has given us with others 'according to what each one needs' (Acts 2: 45). It was in that spirit that Catholics Caring was set up in 1984. It has accomplished much, but it has yet to achieve its full potential. It is not simply another collection. It also calls on Catholics in business and the professions to share their experience, expertise, talents and time with people living in less privileged areas who are our brothers and sisters in Christ. It is not a question just of giving to them but of receiving and learning from them, for they too have much to teach and much to give.

Catholics living in more privileged circumstances should make themselves more aware of the conditions in which their fellow Catholics in more deprived areas live. For them, violence with all its fearful consequences is a daily and a nightly affliction. Unemployment fills many, especially the young, with a sense of hopelessness and failure and resentment. After twenty-one years of suffering, many see no hope of a better future. Those to whom divine providence has been generous must try to find ways of sharing resources, whether of money or time or expertise and skill, with those who have never had a chance. In all this, they must also be aware that many Protestant districts have very similar problems and equally need and deserve support.

Teachers have an important role to play. In sometimes very difficult circumstances they do a magnificent job. In the Catholic schools sector none of us can be complacent about the numbers of pupils who leave our schools without any qualification whatever; we must plan and work together to remedy this situation.

## THE GOOD SHEPHERD

It might be said that I have strayed outside my proper role as pastor or spiritual shepherd. But Christ came to redeem and restore whole persons, and not just souls. He healed bodies as well as souls. People suffering from all kinds of infirmities and afflictions crowded around him. He preached the Good News to the poor and proclaimed liberty to captives. He declared the second great Commandment, 'love your neighbour as yourself' as 'like to the first': 'love the Lord your God'. He taught us to pray to God as 'Our Father', Father of all men and women without any excluded groups; and to pray that His will be done here on earth as it is in heaven. He called himself the Good Shepherd, who knew each of his flock intimately by name and took care of them in every sort of trial.

Christ continued and fulfilled the teaching of the Old Testament prophets. He re-echoed the teaching of Isaiah:

> Hanging your head like a reed,
> lying down in sackcloth and ashes?
> Is that what you call fasting,
> a day acceptable to the Lord?

> Is not this the fast that pleases me
> – it is the Lord who speaks –
> to break unjust fetters
> and undo the thongs of the yoke,

> to let the oppressed go free,
> and break every yoke,
> to share your bread with the hungry,
> and shelter the homeless poor.
> [Isaiah 58:5–7]

I had written the above text before I had a chance to read the booklet *For God and His Glory Alone* (1988) a document prepared by a group of Evangelicals 'from a variety of church fellowships' and intended as 'a contribution relating some biblical principles to the situation in Northern Ireland'. This is a highly significant and most timely publication and is to be commended for study, discussion and action to both Catholics and Protestants in our community. In concluding this chapter, I gladly make my own some words from this publication on the themes of repentance and justice.

First, on justice the document says:

> Because God is a God of Justice, there cannot be anything other than a counterfeit peace when society is built on injustice. Any society which is influenced by Christian principles will be concerned with justice as a priority. Working for peace means working for justice.
>
> *It means:*
> - That we are opposed to any form of religious discrimination in the workplace.
> - That we strive to preserve a judiciary which is respected by the entire community so that justice is not only dispensed but seen to be dispensed with total impartiality.
> - That we work for the removal of unjust structures and patterns in society and specifically those which hurt the poor and the powerless.
> - That we expect those who enforce the law to be answerable to the same principles of justice as the rest of society.
>
> [*For God and His Glory Alone*, ECONI, PO Box 2, Holywood, Co. Down, 1988, p. 12]

Then on repentance the Evangelicals say:

> The only way we can become a community of hope is if we come to God (and to one another) in humility, penitence and repentance. Many in Northern Ireland are caught in a face-saving exercise, but there can be no face-saving at the Cross. The essential nature of repentance is losing face.
>
> We need to say we have been wrong – not merely that we

have been the victims of history. We all need to ask for forgiveness from God and our neighbours, repenting and seeking the way of non-violence and the way of the Cross as the effective means of change in our land. However difficult it may be, we as Christians are committed to Christian means as well as Christian ends. [*Ibid.*, p. 12]

# 7
## SECURITY POLICY AND
## THE SEARCH FOR PEACE

This chapter is in two parts. Part One outlines some of the main considerations that should be reflected in a Christian evaluation of security policy in Northern Ireland. Part Two includes a selection of the statements I have made on major specific issues of security policy during the last ten years.

## PART ONE
### GENERAL CONSIDERATIONS

*The moral law, guardian of human rights, protector of the dignity of man, cannot be set aside by any person or group or by the State itself, for any cause, not even for security or in the interests of law and order. The law of God stands in judgement over all reasons of State. As long as injustices exist in any of the areas that touch upon the dignity of the human person, be it in the political, social or economic field, be it in the cultural or religious sphere, true peace will not exist. The causes of inequalities must be identified through a courageous and objective evaluation, and they must be eliminated so that every person can develop and grow in the full measure of his or her humanity.* [Pope John Paul II, Address at Drogheda, 29 September 1979; in *The Pope in Ireland*, pp. 20–1]

The above section of the Pope's address at Drogheda received very little prominence and almost no comment in British reports. Yet one has to say that one of the urgent needs in Northern Ireland is to accelerate the process of reform that is necessary if the police and the security forces, the judicial and the legal and the prison systems are to receive the confidence of both communities. It is a cliché, but in our situation it is vital truth, that justice must both be done and be manifestly and consistently seen to be done. Urgent though the need and great the desire of the majority of people in both communities to end paramilitary violence, there must be no dilution of the due process of law for that end. This would only defeat its object. It would bring the law itself into discredit. It would, in the words of one commentator, merely 'sow the seeds of another bitter harvest' of violence in the future.

Particular security policies are sometimes claimed to be necessary and right for victory over terrorism. But terrorism is not solely or even primarily a military problem. Victory over it is not to be calculated in terms of military success. Terrorism or revolutionary violence is primarily a political, social, cultural, socio-psychological problem. Unless government policies are successful in these fields, no military successes will amount to 'victory'. The problem in Northern Ireland is basically one of building or restoring trust between the unionist and the nationalist, the Catholic and the Protestant communities: in a word, of reconciliation; it is one of creating confidence between alienated sections of the public and the security forces; of restoring credibility to the legal and judicial system and to political processes and institutions; it is one of tackling unemployment, poverty and urban decay, of redressing alienation, especially among the young. It is, at this moment more than ever, a problem of proving that government has a human heart. Otherwise, to use words from one of the encyclicals of Pope John Paul II, government merely shows itself as 'cold and impersonal justice', its firmness takes on the appearance of 'an oppression of the weak by the strong', its policies have the effect of prolonging 'an arena of permanent struggle of one group against the other' (Pope John Paul II, *Dives in Misericordia*, CTS, London, 1980, p. 74).

Reviews of security policy are frequently called for and in fact undertaken. Often, however, these reviews have to do with the military efficiency of the policies. What is still more necessary is a radical review of their long-term effects, because this is what determines their ultimate effectiveness. There is ample ground for concern. Too many innocent and peaceloving people, and above all too many people from underprivileged backgrounds, are being driven by British Army and security policies into bitterness and hatred, for one to be complacent. There is too much evidence of the British Army's 'leaning heavily' on people from certain addresses, from certain social, cultural or political backgrounds, carrying certain family names, for one not to be raising questions. There must be no handle given to suspicion of double standards in security activity, whether between working-class people and middle-class people, working-class and middle-class residential areas, educated and less educated persons, Catholics and Protestants. There should be a studied avoidance of class or political or national prejudice in the application in Britain of the Prevention of Terrorism Act. In the Northern Ireland tragedy, the Irish people in Ireland are not a guilty people. Irish people in Britain are not a guilty people. Nationalist people in Northern Ireland are not a guilty people. A community, still more a whole people, must not be tarred with the guilt of a minute fraction of the population.

Government must not let itself be pressurised into excessive or exclusive concentration on military and police aspects of security. An integral security strategy includes many more dimensions than military and police ones. Among these are the need to press forward vigorously with economic and industrial redevelopment, job creation, the elimination of inequality and of all discriminatory practices in employment, the rapid replacement of substandard housing, increased budgets for education, particularly for under-achievers, continuing improvement in the legal and judicial system, and a continuing and consistent policy of compassion towards prisoners. It is a serious mistake to look on such measures as 'going soft on terrorism'. The greatest mistakes that have been made by successive British administrations in the past twenty-one years have been those which resulted from the belief that there were quick, effective, 'relentless and resolute' military and police methods of eliminating violence in Northern Ireland. We are still living with the disastrous consequences of such counterproductive measures.

It would be a strange kind of countersubversion that would give subversives precisely what they want. Government should deny them that satisfaction. Government should instead press on with a policy of prudent clemency towards prisoners, in terms of prison conditions, parole, remission and release dates. Compassion is an essential element in any humane, and especially in any Christian, penal system. Clemency is a greater threat to the IRA than harsh repression.

There are repeated calls for the reintroduction of selective internment. All the signs are that the IRA are ready for internment and would welcome it. They do not fear it from the point of view of their paramilitary organisation. They would welcome it as a boost to their sagging political hopes. I venture to say that there are few things that would be more likely to prolong violence for another twenty years.

Those responsible for security, whether at government level or on the ground, must always remember that unlawful violence could never be overcome by unlawful violence on the part of the upholders of law. Security personnel must always act scrupulously within the law and in accordance with the principle of minimum force.

Security forces must always be accountable to the law. No branch of the security forces can be instructed or permitted to act outside the law or can be exempted from accountability to the law of the land. There must be independent and impartial investigation of all incidents of suspected departure by security forces from the restraints of law.

It must also be stated that the security forces, and specifically British Army personnel, however highly trained in military techniques, too often show little evidence of training in the non-military skills essential in dealing with civilians – the arts of sensitivity to community feelings, civility and respect for personal dignity. Too often there is evidence of behaviour, gestures and language that are offensive and insulting, and of attitudes to and treatment of members of the public, and particularly the young, that alienate people from the security forces rather than earn respect for them. It should be a cardinal principle of security policies in Northern Ireland that the IRA campaign of violence will never be overcome by military methods alone. These must be part of and accompanied by a persevering and

142

many-faceted policy of earning respect from the nationalist community for the forces of security and the processes of law. It was a unionist newspaper that wrote recently, in reference to policing:

> The support which the police need, and have a right to expect, in their efforts to bring the murderers to justice, will be forth-coming when people who live in difficult areas have confidence in security procedures. [*News Letter*, 19 August 1988]

Those responsible for security forces training and discipline must never relax in their efforts to have that principle inculcated and observed at all levels and ranks of the security forces.

The use of plastic bullets, or baton rounds, is more than questionable in this context. Indeed the Catholic Bishops of Ireland have pronounced their use morally indefensible. Plastic bullets have killed innocent and uninvolved people. These are potentially lethal weapons and extremely ill-designed for use as methods of riot control. If their use can be justified at all, it could be only as a last resort, in extreme and rare circumstances, and in face of real physical danger to security personnel, and then only on explicit orders from senior officers on the spot and with the utmost care not to inflict serious physical damage or endanger life. Police officers should know that they will be held accountable to the law for improper use of these weapons. Research must be actively pursued into more acceptable and non-lethal methods of riot control.

## POLICING

Policing that is fully answerable to the law, which is impartial, professional, efficient and caring, is an essential condition of justice in any society. When policing breaks down, it is the weakest and the innocent who suffer, the aged, the housebound, children and young people. In many areas, particularly in cities and towns, and particularly in what we used to call working-class areas (which sadly now are too often pools of unemploy-ment), ordinary policing has broken down to a disturbing extent. The result is that the quality of life has been seriously damaged, through the almost uncontrolled social epidemic of car-stealing, mugging, robbery and burglary, vandalism and general misbehaviour on the part of a lawless minority. These communities have a right in justice to normal policing.

It is the universal perception of priests and of people and of community leaders in areas like west and north Belfast that the police are not doing enough to free the streets from crime and to respond promptly to incidents of ordinary as distinct from paramilitary crime. It is also the common perception in such areas that both British Army and police personnel too often deal with civilians, and particularly with young people, in a manner lacking in due courtesy and sensitivity. Too often, insensitive behaviour on the part of members of the security forces corresponds only too closely to the image the IRA seek to attach to the security forces and thus serves the purposes of IRA propaganda.

I have often acknowledged the acute dangers to which the security forces are exposed and the immense difficulties they daily and hourly face as they go about their task in streets where almost any rooftop or corner may conceal a sniper or any wall may screen a grenade-thrower or any culvert hide a bomb. But in the struggle against IRA violence the winning of community goodwill and confidence is as important as any military success. The IRA campaign relies just as much on propaganda as it does on guns and explosives. Too often the IRA are gratuitously being offered ready material for their propaganda war.

The RUC have undoubtedly made sincere efforts in many aspects of policing to act and to be seen to act as a professional body, impartially serving both communities. This has been at the cost of great sacrifice to themselves. Few police forces anywhere have had to operate in more difficult conditions or have suffered heavier casualties in the call of duty.

But given the history of our society and its continuing political polarisation, impartial policing is not going to be achieved easily or quickly. It is a task demanding long, hard, patient and persevering effort. There must be no slackening in that effort.

The achievement of fully impartial policing is in the interests of both communities and must be the aim of both communities. It requires commitment from both communities.

Nationalists must be ready to acknowledge the reforms that have occurred and the undoubted commitment of the RUC to continuing progress towards impartial policing. Such acknowledgement of progress, when it occurs, as well as being merited and due will be an encouragement to further reforms and will lend more credibility to criticisms of the slowness of reform when these criticisms are deserved.

The new code of conduct for the RUC states admirably the principles governing the kind of policing needed in areas like west Belfast. Continuing effort, constant vigilance and earnest self-criticism are needed on the part of the RUC, both operationally and at the level of training, to ensure that police behaviour on the ground corresponds at all times to the high ideals delineated in these admirable paragraphs in the RUC's own code of professional policing ethics:

> If the Royal Ulster Constabulary is to continue to be effective, it must be responsive to the needs and problems of the community it serves. Good relations with the community are also one of the most important prerequisites to the successful discharge of a policeman's duty and it is incumbent upon all members to avail of every opportunity to help reconcile and heal the divisions in the community. The public must also be aware of the problems and difficulties faced by a police officer when discharging his duty in accordance with the law.
>
> The Royal Ulster Constabulary will uphold the law and enforce it to the best of its professional ability, honestly and justly, without favour or affection, malice or ill-will, without regard to status, sex, race, religion or political beliefs and aspirations, whilst understanding and recognising the sensitivities involved. Law enforced in this manner is the citizen's surest guarantee of protection and justice within this community. [RUC, *Professional Policing Ethics*, chapter 1.3]

In the measure, but only in the measure, in which the community's perception of police performance comes to coincide more closely with these aspirations, the RUC will eventually succeed in its aim of winning confidence and co-operation from both sides of the community.

It should be recognised by all that the police and the security forces operate in circumstances of exceptional difficulty and danger. Security personnel have the same reactions and feelings as others have. They can feel nervousness and fear and tension as we all do. Hostility towards them provokes an answering hostility from them. Hate sadly draws forth hate in others, anger stimulates anger in others. Hostility, hatred and anger are never proper attitudes for a follower of Christ.

CRITICISMS OF SECURITY POLICY

Unionist voices are regularly raised calling for 'tougher' security measures, insisting on the 'absolute priority of eradicating terrorism' and calling political initiatives 'bogus' distractions until that aim is first achieved. I ask unionist politicians to believe that constitutional nationalists detest violence and long for its eradication just as much as they do. Constitutional nationalists feel as deep a moral revulsion at the deeds of the IRA as unionists do. Nationalists have suffered through the IRA campaign, and indeed at the hands of the IRA, as much as unionists have. If nationalists express criticisms of security operations or express reservations about restrictive legislation, this is most assuredly not because of any sympathy for men of violence, or from any desire to succour paramilitaries. On the contrary, it is out of genuine concern that certain types of operation and certain kinds of legislation may in fact only serve the interests of the paramilitaries.

THE BROADER ASPECTS OF SECURITY

When Northern Irish nationalists and the Irish government press certain criticisms of security policies, they are not to be dismissed as less than totally committed to the eradication of terrorism. Indeed it is their very concern for the elimination of paramilitarism which urges them to press these points.

Security must be seen in much broader terms than military security.

There is no hope for genuine progress towards security and stability without progress on the socio-economic front, through job creation and fair employment and the amelioration of the quality of life for disadvantaged areas and groups. These measures must not be regarded as bargaining counters or trade-offs for security co-operation. Nor are they to be undertaken simply for political or for security reasons. They are basic requirements of social justice. They are obligations for any government with responsibility for justice and for equality of opportunity for all its citizens. The provision of jobs in west and north Belfast, the protection of existing jobs in east Belfast are the most important steps that government could take towards restoring stability and normality in our society.

## AN ENGLISH PRESBYTERIAN ANALYSIS

I find very relevant observations in a volume entitled *Non Violent Action*, the text of a report prepared by a working party originally set up by the Presbyterian Church in England, now part of the United Reform Church. The report calls attention to the importance of non-violent methods in situations of inter-community tension. It instances the experience of the United Nations (UN) peacekeeping force in Cyprus, where some 4,000 men had notable success in maintaining peace between the Greek and Turkish communities, by reliance mainly on non-violent methods. The report quotes Brigadier Harbottle as saying that the UN force was 'enmeshed' in the ordinary communal life around it. The brigadier remarked, 'Its weapons are negotiation, mediation, quiet diplomacy, tact and patient reasoning, and, above all, an understanding of the human relations involved and of the structural causes of the conflict.' I find these words of astonishing relevance to the security situation in Northern Ireland, across the whole range of security force operations and in the prison service. They could well be framed and displayed in every operations room, briefing centre and prison governor's office.

The same English Presbyterian report gives a series of examples from modern history of successful uses of non-violent methods in averting or eliminating violence and in peacefully promoting just political aims. These should be studied by paramilitary republicans. They deserve to be examined by security planners. They are more relevant to the problems of violence in both parts of Ireland than are calls to develop tougher and more heavily armed 'anti-terrorist' units.

The report analyses the causes of violence in general. Among the causes it enumerates are the following:

(1) Violence arises from fear and anxiety.

(2) Violence is intensified by the example of violence . . . the exposure to violence through the mass media has dangerous implications. Our culture finds it easier to focus on violent behaviour than on its opposite . . .

(3) Violence arises from social injustice . . .

(4) Violence arises from people's sense that they have no effective say in their own destiny . . . If democracy is to be more than a meaningless catchword, there must be some form of responsible participation in decision-making processes . . .

(5) Violence arises from infringement of human rights . . .

(6) Violence arises from a clash of nationalisms . . .

These factors are nowhere more operative in the causation of violence than in Northern Ireland.

Turning to Northern Ireland itself, this report, by a Protestant Church, observes:

The British Army could not succeed as a peace-keeping force for several reasons. First, it was by definition on one side in the conflict. It is ironical that the Army which initially was largely protecting Catholics from Protestant violence, soon became the target of Catholic violence; yet this was inevitable in the situation. Secondly, it responded to violence with violence, and this provoked counter-violence from the IRA. Thirdly, the policy of internment, forced upon a reluctant Army Command, did not put an end to violence, and the misuse of internment powers

became a major factor in driving moderate Catholics away from
a central position, and sometimes into the arms of the IRA . . .

## THE POLITICS OF MERCY

A Churchman who suggests that there is a place in security
and policing policies for mercy would be likely to be dismissed
as naive and romantic, lacking in hard-headed realism. Yet it
must be soberly stated that the people, indeed the only people,
who have succeeded in changing the course of history without
increasing the sum of human suffering have been the people
who practised the works of mercy and love rather than those
who worked war and violence. The men and women of mercy
and love are the only people who, in this present time, are
giving the human race some reason to go on hoping and go on
trying. Decisions and acts that mediate mercy and love would,
I believe, be more relevant to Northern Ireland's immediate
problems now than decisions and acts designed to show grim
firmness and power. What is being asked for is not compromise
of principle, but just enough movement to enable and to evoke
movement from the other side. This, I am convinced, would
also show more real strength and require more authentic
courage.

Mercy and compassion are not weak, ineffectual and impractical. They are dynamic forces for creative change. Christianity's chief contribution to the political process and to the
craft of statesmanship was precisely the dimension of mercy. It
is not for nothing that when Europe was Christian, warring
was forbidden on holy days and during holy seasons, which
were kept for 'the truce of God'. It was not by accident that
the prerogative of the sovereign was pardon, and this pardon
was called 'grace'. Christian politics must be characterised by a
readiness to show mercy, based on the conviction that we have
all sinned and need to have mercy shown us.

St Augustine, reflecting on the dramatic conversion of the
Good Thief on Calvary, asks how it came about that the thief
understood in a flash what the learned Jewish doctors of the
law had not understood, and what the disciples of Jesus had

not yet understood, that this crucified Jesus is the Son of God and Saviour. St Augustine represents himself as asking the Good Thief to explain whether he had arrived at his knowledge by studying the Scriptures, but he receives the answer, 'I did not study the Scriptures; but He looked at me, and in His look, I understood everything.' Christians should look at the face of Jesus, the Man of Sorrows, and ask him to teach us and all those concerned in the Northern Ireland suffering the ways of his mercy.

## PART TWO
### SPECIFIC ISSUES

#### THE EVENTS OF SUNDAY 12 AUGUST 1984
#### IN WEST BELFAST

(On Sunday 12 August 1984 in west Belfast one man, Sean Downes, was killed and several others were injured during a police operation to arrest a Noraid leader who had breached an exclusion order to appear at a march to mark the anniversary of internment.)

The terrible events that occurred in the course of the march in west Belfast on Sunday 12 August 1984 have done a disastrous disservice to the cause of peace in our community. The behaviour of the police, which has been well publicised, bears little sign of that restrained and disciplined use of minimum and reasonable force that is the recognised mark of proper policing. The display of force and the use of force by the police cannot be said to have been justified by the behaviour of the crowd, or to have been in proportion to it.

That Sunday's gathering was not a riot in the accepted meaning of that term. To use words from Lord Scarman's report on the Brixton disorders of 1981, there was by no means 'evidence of a tumultuous, violent crowd determined to execute, and executing a common purpose to attack the police with alarming and very dangerous missiles'. The stated purpose of

150

the police exercise, namely to apprehend a person against whom an exclusion order had been issued, could not justify actions so menacing to life and limb as those taken by the police.

The question must of course be asked, and it must be answered, as to why this exclusion order was issued at all. Surely it could have been foreseen that it would merely serve to attract undue attention to the person's visit, and to enhance its publicity value, thus greatly increasing its propaganda opportunity for the organisers of the visit. Surely it should have been realised that its enforcement would impose an impossible task on the police and create exactly the kind of explosive situation that did result. It must also be asked what orders were given to the police in respect of his apprehension, and by whom; and to what extent the police conformed to those orders.

One young man, Sean Downes, has been tragically killed. I extend my deep sympathy to the grief-stricken widow and family. Many others have been injured. Independent witnesses and news reporters have been shocked and profoundly perturbed by what they saw. Widespread indignation has been aroused, even among moderate and peaceloving people who are totally opposed to paramilitary violence.

These events are a severe setback to the efforts that were declared to be in progress on the part of the RUC to improve relations between the police and the public and to tackle the glaring need to build up among the nationalist population the credibility of the police and confidence in their impartiality.

These events also constitute a new and most grievous setback to the efforts which have undoubtedly been in progress to improve Anglo-Irish relationships and to make political progress towards peace.

The only beneficiaries of Sunday's happenings are those whose energies are devoted to stoking the fires of hate and violence in the community. The sufferers are those who carry on the difficult task of working towards reconciliation and peace.

## An independent inquiry

It was Lord Scarman who said, speaking of police in England

in the aftermath of the Brixton disorders: 'There is a wide-spread and dangerous lack of public confidence in the existing system for handling complaints against the police. By and large, people do not trust the police to investigate the police' (Lord Scarman, *The Brixton Disorders, 10–12 April 1981*, section 5. 43). In Northern Ireland, these words have a special relevance. An independent public inquiry must be set up to investigate the whole episode, apportion responsibilities and make firm recommendations that might go some way towards retrieving the situation.

In the meantime, it should be noted that the dead young man's widow and family strongly deny that he was engaged in riotous behaviour. Imputations should not be cast upon his name, unless indisputable evidence is produced to substantiate the charges.

IRA PROPAGANDA

The platform presentation of the Noraid leader was an obviously provocative act and a blatant publicity stunt designed to secure support at home and in the USA for the murderous purposes of the IRA. The scene was set to secure maximum media coverage for police reaction. It is deplorable that the police should have provided precisely the material desired for the IRA propaganda machine.

REVIEW OF SECURITY AND POLITICAL POLICIES

Some good could still come out of this disaster if it were to lead to a searching review of the whole range of security policies in Northern Ireland. It is time to ask whether the established patterns of deployment and activity of security forces personnel, while they may be securing strictly limited successes in the short term, are doing so at the price of alienating large sections of the community, particularly among the youth, and thus ensuring increased recruitment for paramilitary groups and support for violent policies.

Sunday's events lend greater urgency than ever to the search for political solutions. Another tragic Sunday in Derry in 1972 caused the British government to undertake a radical reappraisal of its whole Northern Ireland policy. Similar courage and similar vision are called for from that government at the present time.

## PLASTIC BULLETS

This tragedy raises again in acute form the question of the use by security forces of plastic bullets. The Catholic bishops, in a statement on 4 July 1983, declared that the use of plastic bullets is morally indefensible and called for their withdrawal as a riot control weapon. In May 1981 the European Parliament called on member states of the European Community to ban the use of plastic bullets. A former chief of the London Metropolitan Police, Sir David McNee, described the plastic bullet as 'alien to the British tradition of policing by consent'. Lord Scarman said:

> I recognise the importance and necessity . . . that such equipment as water cannon, CS gas and plastic bullets should be available in reserve to police forces: however, such equipment should not, I suggest, be used except in a grave emergency – that is, in circumstances in which there is a real apprehension of loss of life. [*The Brixton Disorders*, section 5. 74]

The use of plastic baton rounds for crowd control should now be formally and finally renounced. They have already caused many deaths and a multitude of injuries. They are lethal weapons. They are most certainly destructive of efforts to create community confidence in the police force. In the context of Northern Ireland, whatever reduces community confidence in the police amounts to bad policing.

No responsible person will deny the need and the right and the duty of the police to uphold the rule of law and to defend themselves from attack. The police have to do this in extremely difficult and dangerous conditions. Many of their members and reservists have been brutally murdered in the most callous circumstances. Whether on the streets or in their own homes, they live in constant danger of losing their lives. Their calling and their training, however, demand the strictest discipline in the use of only minimum and reasonable force, whether in law enforcement or in self-defence. To make the law respected is the essential condition for effective law enforcement.

### THE CHRISTIAN LAW OF LOVE AND FORGIVENESS

I appeal to Catholics to keep calm in these tense days and to be guided by Christ's Gospel of love and forgiveness, rather than listen to the raucous voices of hatred and violence. I ask all to pray for the repose of Sean Downes's soul and for God's comforting for his heartbroken widow, Brenda, and his parents and family, and to pray for his orphaned little girl, Clare.

I hope that these events will not blind people to the moral evil of murder perpetrated by paramilitary organisations. I hope that more and more people will come to see that it is precisely the Catholic communtiy that is itself the first and the greatest sufferer from the violence purporting to be conducted for its 'liberation'. I hope that Irish-Americans will not be seduced into providing money for guns that will be used to perpetrate horrible murders and to wreak violence that is poisoning the whole quality of life among nationalist communities. I hope that they will realise that guns in the hands of paramilitary organisations have been used to attack and kill soldiers of Ireland's national army and members of the Garda Síochána of the Irish Republic. What we need from our American friends is not dollars for guns but dollars for jobs.

I also ask all Catholics not to let anything deflect us from our common Christian duty of working non-violently for justice and for peace. We must and we shall never desist from our efforts to promote good relations between ourselves and the Protestant community. We must and we shall never grow weary in our prayer and our work for that peace of Christ which, in every Mass, we are commissioned to share with one another and to spread throughout our whole community.

## THE STALKER–SAMPSON AFFAIR

(Extracts from a homily given in Holy Cross Church, Ardoyne, on 7 February 1988. In 1988 the decision was announced that no action would be taken against members of the RUC whose alleged pursuit of a 'shoot-to-kill' policy had been the subject of the Stalker–Sampson Report.)

The issues raised by the British Attorney General's conclusions on the Stalker–Sampson Report and the decision of the Director of Public Prosecutions (DPP) not to prosecute are of profound and far-reaching importance, not only for Anglo-Irish relations but also for Britain's own interests and for Britain's reputation and standing internationally. It is Britain's own institutions, her self-image and her international image that are at issue.

The two bedrock rules of the British Constitution are the supremacy of Parliament and the rule of law. The great Dicey formulated them a century ago. Regarding the rule of law, Dicey declared, as quoted by Lord Hailsham during the week:

> It means, in the first place, the absolute supremacy or predominance of ordinary law as opposed to the influence of arbitrary power, and excludes the existence of arbitrariness, of prerogative, or even of wide discretionary authority on the part of government.
>
> It means again equality before the law, or the equal subjection of all classes to the ordinary law of the land administered by the ordinary law courts. *The rule of law in this sense excludes the idea of any exemption of officials or others from the duty of obedience to the law which governs other citizens or from the jurisdiction of the ordinary tribunals.* [*Independent*, 3 February 1988, my emphasis]

Lord Hailsham claims that the rulings of the Attorney General and the DPP in the Stalker–Sampson affair 'neither disregarded precedents nor flouted the limitations' indicated in Dicey. In a significant sentence, however, Lord Hailsham concludes his article with the words, 'If they did, the House of Commons has the power to take them to task.'

The principle of the sovereignty of Parliament is, in the British system, parallel to the principle of the rule of law. Parliament is the custodian and ultimate guarantor of the rule of law. With respect to the advice that led to the decision not to prosecute, the Attorney General is answerable to Parliament. It is most earnestly to be hoped that the House of Commons will not fail in its duty to probe this grave matter to its depths.

There must be full parliamentary scrutiny of the Attorney General's and the DPP's invocation in this case of 'matters concerning the public interest and considerations of national security'. Whatever independent inquiry is needed to establish the truth should be instituted.

There could be no more serious charges brought against a policeman than that of first carrying out or authorising the shooting dead of unarmed and untried men – whatever the suspicions entertained or even, in some of the cases, the facts known, about them – and second of 'perverting or attempting or conspiring to pervert the course of justice or obstructing a constable in the execution of his duty'. A police force in which men responsible for such activities continued to be serving officers could never win for itself the confidence of the community.

*The Economist* of 4 February 1988 says:

> The British Government is too protective of its police and far too fond of hushing things up. It could start to put these faults right, in the longer term by outlawing uncorroborated confessions, and at once by publishing the Stalker–Sampson inquiry's report, however high its findings may strike.

Decisions of such gravity as these are scarcely likely to have been made at RUC level alone. Some of them must surely have been made or formally cleared at high government level. It is vitally important that responsibilities be ascribed where they belong. Subordinates must not be made scapegoats for decisions of higher authority.

I believe that, under the leadership of Sir John Hermon, courageous efforts have been made and considerable progress achieved in forming the RUC into a non-partisan, impartial and professional police force and in improving the image of the force in the eyes of a substantial section of the nationalist community. All this hard-won progress can be destroyed unless satisfactory solutions are found to the present debacle.

I believe in the integrity and fair-mindedness of the Secretary of State, Mr Tom King, and in his commitment to fair treatment for the nationalist community. But the work he has been trying to do can be most seriously damaged unless the many and grave questions raised by the Stalker–Sampson affair are satisfactorily resolved.

## Anglo-irish confidence

Anglo-Irish relations have been severely damaged by this affair. It is essential for both countries that confidence be restored. Relations between Britain and Ireland must not be limited to the single issue of security co-operation. That issue is certainly important, but it cannot be isolated from its total context of mutual trust between two governments and two police forces, trust in the integrity of commitments given, trust in the legal institutions under which the security forces operate, and total subjection of the security forces to the rule of law.

No one should deny the necessity of combating paramilitary violence. No one should underestimate the difficulties and the dangers faced by the security forces in doing so. No one should forget the great sacrifices and heavy losses suffered by the RUC in this task. But let no one suppose that the struggle against paramilitarism can be won by security operations alone, least of all by 'fire-power, speed and aggression'.

Above all, let no one suppose that the struggle can be won by setting aside or bending the rule of law. On the contrary, paramilitarism can be successfully countered only by security forces that operate and are seen at all times to operate unambiguously under the rule of law. To quote Lord Hailsham again:

> I do not accept the view that there is any legal justification for criminal or tortious activity by the security services, either at common law or by virtue of the Royal Prerogative . . . In English

law, members of the security services are as much subject to the laws of homicide, assault, perjury, conspiracy or even trespass as any other of Her Majesty's subjects. [*Independent*, 3 February 1988]

The gaining by the RUC of the respect and confidence of the nationalist community is an essential condition for its success in overcoming paramilitary violence. That respect and confidence can be gained only by absolute respect for the rule of law on the part of the RUC and by their own impartial enforcement of the law. It is in the interests of the RUC itself that the truth about this sordid affair be officially established at Parliament and government level and that responsibility and guilt be ascribed where they belong. The Stalker affair will not go away. Only when truth is told and justice is done can the affair be left behind.


JUSTICE, TRUTH AND PEACE

It might be objected that what I have been saying is out of place in a church at Mass. This is not so. Mass includes prayer for peace and commitment to work for peace. All that I have said is directly related to the search for peace. There is no peace without truth and justice. The German Lutheran theologian Jürgen Moltmann said in a recent lecture: 'Peace is not absence of violence but the presence of justice. It is justice which creates peace, not vice versa, and so every act of justice is an act of peace' (the *Tablet*, 9 January 1988). Psalm 71 foretells the kingdom of peace that will be ushered in by the Christ who is to come. It says:

In his days justice shall flourish
and peace till the moon fails,
he shall rule from sea to sea,
from the Great River to earth's bounds.

The psalm undoubtedly points forward to Jesus Christ, 'the father of the world to come, the Prince of Peace'. The Preface of the feast of Christ the King says:

As King Christ claims dominion over all creation
that he may present to you, his Almighty Father
an eternal and universal Kingdom,
a Kingdom of truth and life
a Kingdom of holiness and Grace,
a Kingdom of justice, love and peace.

We pray in this Mass and in every Mass for peace, true peace, just peace, peace in our day, that peace which is a forerunner of the unity and peace of God's eternal kingdom, where Christ, Our Lord, lives and reigns with the Father and the Holy Spirit for ever and ever. Amen.

### THE RELEASE OF PRIVATE THAIN

(Extracts from a homily given in Holy Trinity Church, Belfast, 28 February 1988. In 1984 Private Ian Thain was found guilty of the murder of a civilian in Northern Ireland and sentenced to life imprisonment. After serving three years of his sentence he was released on licence by the Home Secretary and reinstated in his British Army regiment.)

On 11 August 1983 I assisted in Holy Trinity Church, Belfast at the funeral Mass for Thomas 'Kidso' Reilly, who had been shot dead by a soldier two days earlier. He was a young man aged twenty-two from Ardmonagh Gardens, who had been travelling all over Ireland and Britain as a pop group road manager. He was a young man with no political involvement and no connection with any paramilitary organisation. His killing aroused intense resentment in the whole neighbourhood. An immediate investigation was promised and instituted by the British Army.

The soldier in question, Private Ian Richard Thain, who was eighteen years of age at the time of the shooting, was brought to trial in Belfast Crown Court in December 1984. He was found guilty of murder and given a life sentence. Private Thain was the first serving British soldier to be so sentenced while on duty in Northern Ireland in the twenty-one years since the Troubles began.

The accused had claimed that he fired in self-protection, because he had reason to believe that Thomas was carrying a gun and was about to draw it. The trial judge found, however, that Private Thain had 'concocted the defence', and had been 'deliberately untruthful' when it suited him. The judge declared: '[This] confirms my conclusion that the accused had no honest belief that the deceased was about to draw a gun and shoot him.' The judge said that he had taken into account the soldier's youth and inexperience and the fact that at the relevant time he had been suffering from lack of sleep. Nevertheless, the judge declared that he did not accept that the accused had been suffering from emotional shock or reaction, and pointed out that the soldier had not warned colleagues about the possible presence of a gun. Private Thain was found guilty of murder and sentenced to life imprisonment.

The trial and the verdict seemed at the time to carry the clear message that security forces personnel were never to be allowed to see themselves as being above the law and were at all times to be and to be seen to be amenable to the law in the exercise of their duty.

All the greater, therefore, were the amazement and the incredulity evoked last week by the news that Private Thain, after serving only three years of a life sentence, had been released on a licence from the Home Secretary; and, more astonishing still, had been reinstated in his army regiment. On 24 February 1988 the *Daily Telegraph* called the whole event an act of 'gross insensitivity'. In a leading article, this newspaper, normally supportive of the Conservative government, goes on to say: 'What is incomprehensible is the man's recall to his unit, an act of such stunning insensitivity that we find it hard to imagine what the Ministry of Defence was thinking of.' I do not criticise the principle of clemency in such a case. However, the Thain decision needs to be placed in a wider context.

INSENSITIVITY OF RECENT DECISIONS

It is impossible not to place this decision in the context of the series of events which have so seriously harmed Anglo-Irish relations over recent weeks, and which have given such a grievous setback to the credibility of the security forces. The London *Times* links the Private Thain episode with the Stalker inquiry and the decision not to prosecute RUC officers, in spite of evidence of 'perverting or attempting or conspiring to pervert the course of justice or obstructing a constable in the execution of his duty'. *The Times* calls both of these decisions foolish and wrong. It declares editorially: 'These misjudgements are wrong, not because they fail to take into account the views of the Republic: they are simply wrong. In addition, they have serious consequences for public faith in the security forces' (*The Times*, 24 February 1988).

CREDIBILITY OF THE SECURITY FORCES

Perhaps the most depressing aspect of these recent events is that it would seem that the British government has not yet fully grasped that the only way forward out of our stalemate of destruction in Northern Ireland lies through a systematic policy for establishing the conditions of credibility of the political and legal and judicial institutions under which we are governed, together with a patient and planned and methodical policy of building up public confidence that the security forces are non-partisan, politically impartial and fully answerable to the rule of law. Scant respect for the rule of law was surely shown in the Stalker affair, and scant respect for the courts was shown in the Private Thain episode.

It is high time that more evidence was forthcoming of acceptance by the British government that the struggle for hearts and minds is ultimately more important than any purely military success. Indeed, the sustained attempt to gain public confidence in the peaceful process of reform of structures and institutions, and in the effectiveness of the peaceful way to justice, are conditions without which any purely military success would be completely negated by political failure.

Meanwhile, Britain's own international reputation is being put on the line. The credibility of Britain's influence and the

acceptability of her intervention in disputes elsewhere throughout the world is being undermined. It is in Britain's own interest,
domestically and internationally, that she show greater sensitivity to feelings in Ireland, nationalist and unionist alike, and act
consistently up to the measure of her historic responsibility
towards her sister island and in fidelity to the spirit as well as
the letter of her international obligations towards this country.

### THE BIRMINGHAM SIX AND THE CASE OF ANNIE MAGUIRE AND THE LATE GIUSEPPE CONLON

(Extracts from a homily given in Holy Cross Church, Ardoyne,
on 7 February 1988, and from subsequent addresses. The Birmingham Six were sentenced to life imprisonment in 1975 for
the murder of twenty-one people in a series of pub bombings
in Birmingham. For over sixteen years grave doubts had been
cast about the quality of the evidence on which their convictions were based. On 14 March 1991 their second appeal was
allowed and they were released.)

In February 1988 I visited two of the Birmingham Six in
Wormwood Scrubs prison. In September 1990 I visited all of
the Six, who were divided over Gartree Prison and Long Lartin
prison. I have met with many of the relatives of these men.

The conviction of the innocence of the Six that I formed the
first time I met any of them was reinforced in September 1990.
I can see no reason why their convictions should continue to
stand or why they should not be vindicated quickly and released.

Saying Mass for the men in Wormwood Scrubs, I used as
the first reading the following passage from the Book of Job:

Is not man's life on earth nothing more than pressed service,
his time no better than hired drudgery? . . .
months of delusion I have assigned to me,
nothing for my own but nights of grief.
Lying in bed I wonder: 'When will it be day?'
Risen, I think: 'How slowly evening comes!'

... My days have ... vanished
leaving no hope behind.
My eyes will never again see joy.
[Job 7: 1–7]

How sadly apt those chilling words seemed to the situation of the men gathered around the altar that morning. After thirteen years in prison and a long campaign conducted on their behalf by a most dedicated body of journalists, solicitors, barristers, Members of Parliament and clergy, hopes of release had been raised and then bitterly dashed. It was not only the verdict of the Court of Appeal that caused dismay. It was also the total and seemingly almost contemptuous rejection of every part of the case argued for the men by their able counsel. It was also the cold, insensitive and unfeeling way in which the verdict was felt to be delivered. Even learned judges should remember that they are only weak, human and fallible instruments of justice; they are not arbiters of final judgement.

In the course of a long conversation with the two men, what impressed me strongly was their composure, their serenity, their dignity in the face of crushing disappointment, and above all their deep religious faith and their spiritual strength. I had visited the same two men and spoken with them at length on a previous occasion three years ago. I spent three days in the courtroom at the Old Bailey while the Appeal Court hearing was in progress. I have spoken with many persons whose opinion I hold in high regard and who know the Birmingham Six intimately over all the years of their imprisonment.

From these conversations and from my own meetings with the men, I believe that it was their misfortune to be in the wrong place at the wrong time and to be caught in a maze of circumstances that, at that particular time, and given the mood that understandably swept through Britain in the wake of the appalling carnage of Birmingham, looked suspicious and were susceptible to a sinister interpretation, but which were innocent and were all of them capable of a perfectly innocuous interpretation. The men were caught in a web of Kafkaesque concatenations of circumstances, whose every single element

163

had a perfectly innocent explanation, but all of which together carried by association and convergence a specious appearance of guilt.

Many people in Britain as well as in Ireland share my conviction of the men's innocence. That, however, is not my present point. What is important is the widespread unease that persists about the case. Many feel that justice has not been done or been seen to be done. The influential and internationally respected British journal *The Economist* says:

> Respectable bishops, parliamentarians (British and Irish), journalists have ever since been crying that justice miscarried. To placate them, the Home Secretary last year asked the Court of Appeal to consider three options: to order the convicts released; to call a fresh trial; or to let the sentences stand. It let them stand. The men had been tortured. As the Lord Chief Justice of England said: 'There was no doubt they had been violently assaulted in the prison by prison officers and/or prisoners.' But the prison officers charged with injuring them were acquitted, and the men were segregated from other prisoners. It was to the police that they made their confused confessions. As for the forensic evidence, both the validity of the tests and the reliability of the tester were much questioned in court. The Birmingham trial underlines the need to scrap the peculiar willingness of the English courts to accept uncorroborated confessions, which openly invites police abuse. Far too many people are convicted on such evidence alone. [*The Economist*, 4 February 1988]

NO MERE BRITISH-BASHING

The case, however, should not be made the occasion of mere British-bashing. After all, it is people in Britain who have been the main protagonists of the cause of the Six. Were it not for the voices of Church leaders and distinguished figures in public life, were it not for the many men and women of integrity and commitment in the legal profession in Britain and for the tenacity in pursuit of truth and justice of many British journalists and of some Members of Parliament, the case of the Six would never have impinged on the public conscience as it has done.

Were it not for the integrity of the British Home Secretary, it would never have gone to the Court of Appeal.

## IRA GUILT

A major share of the responsibility for the imprisonment of the Six rests here in Ireland. The IRA know who prepared and who planted the Birmingham bombs. The persons who were involved in the outrage and the leaders of their organisation carry guilt for the suffering of the Birmingham Six. They could even now secure their vindication and their release.

## A CASE OF CONSCIENCE FOR BRITAIN

The Birmingham Six case will continue to disturb the consciences of many people in Britain and to damage British interests internationally until justice is seen to be done. It is the British legal system that must accept responsibility for the delivery of justice. No country's legal or judicial system can guarantee that justice is done in every case. The British system is better than most and Britain has made a major contribution, historically and internationally, to the protection of justice through the rule of law and the institutions of law. This is all the more reason why those in Britain who take pride in that tradition and who wish to see it kept beyond all suspicion must continue to take the Birmingham Six case very seriously indeed. The Birmingham Six case is a test case. It will not go away. It must not be allowed to go away. As *The Economist* points out, it demonstrates weaknesses in the British legal system that must be remedied. A Select Committee on Home Affairs in Britain six years ago recommended the setting up of an independent review body to inquire into miscarriages of justice. The Birmingham Six case sharply underlines the urgent need for this independent review.

Meanwhile, the campaign for their release and for the vindication of their innocence must go on and will go on. Anyone who has new evidence relevant to the case should come forward now. Here in Down and Connor, and particularly in Ardoyne and in the Sacred Heart parishes, where five of the Six had their first home, we shall continue to give them the full support of our belief in their innocence and of our prayers and our efforts on their behalf. They are not forgotten. They are no longer alone.

## Postscript

The Birmingham Six have at last been freed and their innocence vindicated. Nothing can adequately compensate them for the multiple injustices they have suffered. Nothing can undo their sixteen years of unjust deprivation of liberty.

If, however, their experience leads, as it must, to radical changes in the system for the administration of criminal law, their suffering will not have been in vain, their place in British legal history will have been assured.

The British legal and judicial process has at least demonstrated that it can within its own structures find ways of detecting and reversing its own miscarriages of justice and correcting its own defects. But sixteen years' unjust imprisonment is an injustice too long suffered and a wrong too late redressed. It will be to the credit of, and will enhance the stature of, British justice if it has the resolution necessary to ensure that other miscarriages of justice are now recognised and remedied and that similar miscarriages are made impossible in the future.

## Annie Maguire and the late Giuseppe Conlon

The quality of the evidence on which Annie Maguire and her friends, including Giuseppe Conlon who died in prison, were convicted of murders in England has been the subject of grave concern. Lengthy prison sentences were served by those convicted and they still campaign for their good names to be restored.

I requested Douglas Hurd when he was the Home Secretary to re-open the case of Mrs Annie Maguire and her friends and of the late Giuseppe Conlon. I am fully convinced of their innocence also. True justice has nothing to lose by subjecting its own processes to rigorous scrutiny by the very standards in the name of which it sits in judgement on wrongdoers.

# 8
## THERE IS NO ALTERNATIVE TO PEACE

In this chapter I wish to add to all that I have said over the years about the moral evil of all paramilitary violence, whether republican or loyalist, some considerations of a more historical and political nature. I believe these considerations to be valid and relevant, but I by no means claim for them the same competence or the same authority that I must as bishop, speaking in union with the Pope and with all the bishops of Ireland, claim for my moral judgement on violence.

The IRA have systematically closed their ears to the Church's moral teaching and refused to be influenced by moral condemnations, exhortations and appeals, whether from Pope or from bishops. Indeed, they regularly accuse bishops of 'talking politics' or 'taking political sides', when instead they are speaking as moral teachers, with a responsibility and an authority derived from Christ.

I put forward the following reflections because I believe that the IRA's apologia for their campaign is based on a reading of history that is selective and a political analysis that is flawed. If the debate that seems to be in progress amongst IRA militants and their supporters were to be stimulated by these reflections, I believe my putting them forward would be worthwhile.

The IRA claim that 'There is no alternative to armed struggle.' I shall attempt to show instead that, even for the IRA, there is no alternative to peace, and that only through peace can the aims of any of the political communities within Northern Ireland be achieved.

Territory and people

The IRA and Sinn Féin reading of Irish history in this century sees the struggle for Irish national independence as having succeeded in 1922 in achieving partial independence for twenty-six counties of Ireland, leaving six counties still 'occupied' by British forces and still ruled by the British Crown. The aims of 1916 were therefore not completed. There is still 'unfinished business'. The present IRA claim that the 'armed struggle' begun in 1916 was called off prematurely and treacherously, before its aims were completed; and that the present 'armed struggle' is a continuation of the earlier one and is vowed to the final and definitive completion of the 'unfinished business'.

There are at least two serious flaws in this version of history. First, the 'armed struggle' of 1916–22 failed in the northeastern counties not because it was prematurely terminated, but because in this corner of Ireland it came up against the hard rock of implacable unionist opposition to union with the rest of the country in an Irish nationalist Ireland. The IRA failed in the northeast because they lacked the mass support and the clear democratic mandate which they enjoyed throughout the rest of the island as a result of the 1918 election. In that election, Sinn Féin secured 73 seats, Home Rule 6 seats, and unionists 26 seats, the latter concentrated in the northeast part of the island. The political division of the country between nationalist and unionist was made clearly evident in that election, and it prefigured and made possible the territorial division which followed.

Martin McGuinness, a prominent Sinn Féin spokesman, has recently written:

> It was partition which drove a wedge between people in this country and impeded the growth of an Ireland where religious differences could be tolerated as simply aspects of a multi-cultural society, as had happened elsewhere throughout the world.

Gerry Adams has more recently spoken of the chaos and division created by the British occupation of part of our country.

Such statements evade the decisive issue, namely that the 'wedge between people in this country' was already there before territorial partition was imposed. The democratic election of 1918, which gave Sinn Féin overwhelming endorsement over the rest of the country, clearly indicated the extent of the wedge and showed the intractable nature of the problems caused by unionist dissent from the nationalist position. Partition was a flawed solution. But Irish national unity at that time was an impossible solution. It was made impossible because of the bitterness of the pre-existent division between the unionist and the nationalist communities. The wedge between the two communities has been vastly widened in the past twenty-one years and the development of a peaceful 'multi-cultural society' immeasurable impeded – principally and precisely because of the 'armed struggle' of the IRA. Partition was and is a symptom and not just the originating cause of the underlying division. The underlying causes are such that armed violence is quite simply invalid and ineffectual as a solution, and indeed produces effects exactly the opposite of those intended.

Undoubtedly, in the 1920s and in the following decades, it suited British imperial interests, militarily, politically and economically, to retain this part of Ireland within the United Kingdom. But it would not have been possible for them to do this without the deep loyalty to the Crown and the unwavering allegiance to the United Kingdom of a million Irish unionists.

The second flaw in the Sinn Féin version of history is that the problems created for nationalists and republicans by mass unionist opposition were such as to be utterly incapable of being resolved by 'armed struggle'. Indeed the republican physical force campaign only intensified unionist opposition. The incorporation of unionists against their will into the new Irish state would have been impossible for even Britain to enforce, much more for the new Irish state to sustain. Of their very nature the problems could have hope of being solved only by patient and prolonged persuasion, through dialogue and the evolution through time of the political process. The armed struggle of 1916 to 1922 failed to incorporate the six northeastern counties into a united and independent Ireland simply because physical force was irrelevant to the central problem. It was based upon a disastrous misreading of the situation. It merely aggravated the problem and compounded and consolidated the division of the country. Of all the ways to reunification, violence is the one way that is guaranteed never to make the goal attainable.

I hasten to add that republican violence was by no means the only, or even the worst, form of violence operating in the North at that time. Loyalist violence and the legalised violence of the security forces, often acting in consort with loyalist gangs, operated a continuous campaign of vicious violence during those sad and bitter years.

Part of the reason for the mistaken republican analysis of the Northern problem was the confusion of territory with people. Because the territory of Ireland was one indivisible island, it was automatically concluded that its inhabitants must be one indivisible people, under one sovereign Irish government. This conclusion was plausible. But the past history and present developments of Europe have proved again and again that national unity cannot be imposed on large dissident minorities by force. It can come about by peaceful evolution, through the democratic process; it will never and can never be imposed through the barrel of the armalite.

The British for their part equally misread the situation and applied a flawed solution. They too confused territory with people. They selected an area large enough to be politically viable but not so large as to endanger the unionist majority within that area. The historical province of Ulster had therefore itself to be partitioned, since the unionist majority in the partitioned area there would not otherwise be secure. In the six counties separated from the rest of Ireland and from the rest of Ulster, it was calculated that the unionist and British majority vote would be unassailable. The British went on to declare the whole of that territory British and unionist, and set up for it political institutions which were exclusively British and unionist. They thereby ignored the existence and the rights of the large Irish nationalist minority within the partitioned territory. By definition, nationalists were excluded from participation in the government of a society which denied their Irishness and their nationalism. They could have a place in government only at unionist pleasure and, in effect, only by abjuring nationalism and becoming unionist.

Thus a second intractable minority was created in Ireland by British policy, however much that policy was made possible and was facilitated by existing conditions in Ireland itself. The nationalist minority in Northern Ireland proved as impossible to conciliate and to assimilate against their will into a unionist Northern Ireland as a Northern unionist minority would have been impossible to conciliate and to assimilate against their will into an Irish nationalist Ireland.

If unionist administrations had pursued policies of conciliation and assimilation, they might have had some chance in the long term of bringing about a stable and reconciled Northern Ireland. As a matter of historical fact, such policies were not pursued. Instead, unionists continued to act as an insecure and threatened minority even within Northern Ireland, seeing their nationalist neighbours as a threat and fearing that any concessions to nationalists would put their own position in peril.

Nationalists, for their part, refused to recognise the legitimacy of the new Northern Ireland state or to participate in its institutions. They pursued a policy of abstention. They went into a kind of internal political exile, waiting for the entity called Northern Ireland to wither away from what they saw as its inherent and unjust arbitrariness and artificiality, and vigorously protesting against its unjust and discriminatory policies on voting rights, its electoral gerrymandering, its discrimination in jobs and in housing.

The situation had all the elements of a great human and social tragedy. Each side behaved exactly as the other needed it to behave in order to justify and to sustain its own perception of the other. Each side behaved in such a way as to lead the other to act at its worst. Each side felt fully justified in its judgement of and attitude towards the other. But since unionists did control all decision-making and did hold a monopoly of political and economic power and privilege, their responsibility for things done and things left undone in respect of the other community was greater.

Meanwhile Britain, having created the situation, devised a classic double-act formula for retaining control while washing its hands of responsibility. If protests were made at Westminster about the policies of the regional government at Stormont, they were declared to be the internal affairs of the Northern Ireland Parliament and government, and not of Westminster.

If these policies were raised internationally or by the Irish government, they were declared to be internal affairs of the United Kingdom, in which no foreign government (where 'foreign' included the Irish government) had any right to interfere.

This posture had eventually to be abandoned when the Northern Ireland government virtually lost control of the situation in the late 1960s and early 1970s and Westminster had once more to assume direct responsibility for the affairs of Northern Ireland. After fifty years of absentee sovereignty over Northern Ireland, the British government again had to try to come to grips directly with the 'unfinished business' of Ireland.

A NEW NATIONALISM

In the aftermath of the Civil Rights Movement and with the foundation of the Social Democratic and Labour Party (SDLP), Northern nationalism undertook a major rethink of its nature, its aims and its policies. Without abjuring its nationalist identity or its aspiration to a united Ireland, nationalism committed itself to pursue its aims exclusively through political dialogue and the democratic process. It definitively rejected abstention and set itself to work within the institutions of Northern Ireland and to work, like other democratic parties, for the internal welfare of Northern Ireland, while continuing peacefully to pursue the long-term objective of a united Ireland in which nationalism and unionism could be eventually reconciled in an agreed Ireland.

This was a historic and indeed dramatic transformation in Irish nationalism. Tragically, unionists, with their inbuilt insecurity, mistrust and suspicion, tended to regard the founding of the SDLP as merely a more slow and subtle form of subversion. This unionist reaction, and the new resurgence in the 1970s of armed republican subversion, combined to bring about the loss, or at least the long deferment, of the chance of an agreed cross-community settlement in Northern Ireland.

THE ANGLO-IRISH AGREEMENT

The British government, meanwhile, now obliged to come closer to grips again after half a century with the Irish problem, carried out a fresh analysis of the problem. The first indications of the results of that analysis were given in a very significant document, published in 1972, to which I referred in chapter 1. For the first time, this document signalled that the British government at last recognised the 'double minority' situation in Ireland as a whole and in Northern Ireland in particular, as being close to the heart of the whole Irish problem, and accepted that institutions must be devised that would correspond to the reality of the two minorities and would attempt to mediate between their respective and competing demands. The two essential elements in British government policy then and since were first adumbrated in that document, namely, devolved government with some form of power-sharing within Northern Ireland, and some form of 'Irish dimension' both within Northern Ireland and in its relationships with the Republic of Ireland. The British government has not fundamentally deviated from that policy since then.

The Anglo-Irish Agreement was already present in embryo in the 1972 Green Paper. The Agreement, signed in 1984, represented a fundamental change in British policy towards Ireland and held promise of a radical transformation of Anglo-Irish relations. The Agreement was an attempt to institutionalise an Irish dimension and at the same time initiate movement towards cross-community agreement on governmental structures for Northern Ireland.

From the point of view of many nationalists, it was a very diluted form of Irish dimension; yet the majority of nationalists were willing to accept it as a step forward towards recognition of the Irish nationalist identity within Northern Ireland. For nationalists, therefore, any reversal of the basic principles of the Anglo-Irish Agreement would be unacceptable.

Unionists from the beginning rejected and opposed the Agreement root and branch. They were justifiably aggrieved that they had not been involved in the negotiations preceding the Agreement. The Agreement itself aroused all their traditional feelings of betrayal and isolation, and their inherited fears of submission and suppression by instalments. Their negative reaction was therefore understandable; it would have been more constructive, however, had it been complemented by an outline by unionists of their alternative to the Anglo-Irish Agreement. It would be an important contribution to inter-community debate if the unionist community were prepared to indicate what shape a replacement for the Agreement should assume, and what steps they would take to make Northern Ireland, in the words of the Ulster Unionist Party document of 1984, a place which nationalists too could feel was theirs.

The unionist community continues to regard Northern Ireland as a place that is foreign territory so far as the Republic of Ireland is concerned and holds that the Republic of Ireland has no right to 'interfere' in the affairs of Northern Ireland. This analysis is as offensive to nationalists as the analysis by republicans of Northern Ireland as 'occupied territory' is offensive to unionists.

For the Republic to regard Northern Ireland as foreign territory would be to repudiate a defining principle of Irish nationalism. Furthermore, it should be recognised that for seventy years the divided state and the recurrent tension and conflict in Northern Ireland have been a source, and indeed the only source, of danger to stability and of internal security problems in the Republic itself. They have required an enormous expenditure on security in the Republic. They constitute at present a burden on the taxpayers of the Republic of Ireland that is relatively far greater than that carried for Northern Ireland by United Kingdom taxpayers. No government in the Republic could ignore the Northern Ireland problem. Whether they wished it or not, Northern Ireland would remain an internal problem in the politics of the Republic.

THE INTERNAL CONTRADICTIONS OF MILITANT REPUBLICANISM

Although this is so, there is total opposition among all constitutional Irish nationalists, both in Northern Ireland and in the Republic, to all use of violence for the furtherance of nationalist aims. This is all the more remarkable and the more significant because of the frequent association of Irish nationalism with violence in the past. The use of violence by the present IRA over the past twenty-one years is totally repudiated by the overwhelming majority of Irish nationalists, both North and South.

The successes of physical force Irish nationalism between 1916 and 1922 were not solely or even primarily military successes. Revolutions succeed or fail not primarily by military means alone, but by the political readiness of the masses of the people for revolution. The military Irish Republican Movement of seventy years ago achieved what success it did because it was backed up by a powerful populist political and revolutionary movement throughout the whole nationalist community. The contrast with the present IRA campaign is glaring. After twenty years of political campaigning the IRA have significantly failed to create a populist revolutionary movement or to secure any significant popular or electoral support, North or South. On these grounds alone their campaign is doomed to fail. At its peak, in the emotional aftermath of the 1980–1 hunger strikes, the Sinn Féin vote in the Republic reached about 9 per cent. It has since fallen steadily and reaches now less than 2 per cent. This is enough to show the absurdity of the claim of the IRA to be 'waging a war of liberation on behalf of the Irish people'.

Indeed the IRA and their political spokespersons seem implicitly themselves to concede failure on this front. In June 1989, Gerry Adams said in Bodenstown, 'The [Sinn Féin] Party has been unable to persuade any sizeable section of the electorate of its relevancy and the desire for change in the Republic has passed Sinn Féin by.' At the 1989 Sinn Féin Ard Fheis it was admitted from the platform, according to reports, that the 'Republican Movement' 'cannot win the struggle for Irish national self-determination on its own', but that 'a broad-based campaign is needed'. One subsequent statement goes so far as to admit: 'We, the Republican Movement, are actively fighting a struggle in the name of the Irish people. The vast majority of those people do not agree with us, so they do not identify with our struggle.'

During the Sinn Féin/SDLP discussions in 1988 and at both the 1989 and 1990 Sinn Féin *ard fheiseanna* and in frequent statements issued in between, Sinn Féin leaders have again and again called for 'a firm, united and unambiguous demand from all Irish national parties for an end to the unionist veto and a declaration of a date for British departure'. They have pleaded for a 'broad-based all-Ireland imperialist mass movement'. A wide variety of descriptions of this 'mass movement' has followed in succession. It has been described as an 'overall nationalist strategy for justice and peace', 'maximum agreement with all the other forces', 'maximum political unity in Ireland', 'the broadest possible alliance', a 'pan-nationalist consensus'.

Strangely, these statements ignore the fact that there is already a 'pan-nationalist consensus', unanimously endorsed by all constitutional political parties in the Republic and by all constitutional nationalist parties in Northern Ireland. All these parties, after months of discussion and research and consultation, succeeded in the difficult task of producing the agreed statement of contemporary Irish nationalism that was endorsed by the New Ireland Forum. This document definitively and unequivocally repudiated violence. To use Sinn Féin terminology, this statement represented an 'overall nationalist strategy for justice and peace', and it achieved 'maximum political unity in Ireland' among all nationalists except Sinn Féin. It is in fact the 'pan-nationalist consensus' concerning the 'primary national aim' of Irish reunification. By this statement, constitutional nationalists unanimously rejected the Sinn Féin analysis of the Northern problem and repudiated the IRA use of violence to achieve the national aim. One trenchant paragraph declared:

> Attempts from any quarter to impose a particular solution through violence must be rejected along with the proponents of such methods. It must be recognised that the new Ireland which the Forum seeks can come about only through agreement and must have a democratic basis. [*Report of the New Ireland Forum*, 5.2(2) p. 27]

The report added:

> The Parties in the Forum will continue to work by peaceful means to achieve Irish unity in agreement. There are many varying constitutional and other structures of political unity to be found throughout the world, for example, Australia, France, Italy, Spain, Switzerland and the United States of America, which recognise to the extent necessary the diversity as well as the unity of the people concerned and ensure constitutional stability. It is essential that any structures for a new Ireland must meet both these criteria.
>
> The particular structure of political unity which the Forum would wish to see established is a unitary state, achieved by agreement and consent, embracing the whole island of Ireland and providing irrevocable guarantees for the protection and preservation of both the unionist and nationalist identities. A unitary state on which agreement had been reached would also provide the ideal framework for the constructive interaction of the diverse cultures and values of the people of Ireland. [*Ibid.*, 5.6, 5.7]

Sinn Féin stand self-excluded from this pan-nationalist consensus. Their support for violence is the paramount reason for their exclusion from the consensus of the Irish nationalist community in general. They will continue to be excluded from the Irish nationalist community so long as they continue supporting that campaign of violence. It may be that the confined circles in which they move and the limited contacts which they have insulate them from the feeling of the nationalist population in general. It may be that they do not wish to face reality. The fact is that they seem not even to be aware of the deep moral revulsion their campaign arouses in the vast majority of Irish nationalist people all over Ireland, North and South. They do not seem to realise that their activities have made the republican name and cause odious in the minds of many and have for very many Irish nationalist people turned a proud and honoured name and cause into a matter of shame.

Here is located the central internal contradiction in the movement. This is the stark dilemma the Sinn Féin/IRA movement must confront. The contradiction is inherent in their attempt to operate a dual strategy, political and military, where the two strategies mutually negate each other. Already in 1977 at Bodenstown, the Sinn Féin leadership declared that the IRA 'could not militarily defeat the British Army' without an accompanying political struggle. But the more the IRA escalate the 'military' campaign, as they have notoriously been doing recently, they erode their hopes of retaining, much more of expanding, their already slender political base, and the deeper they travel into the political wilderness, isolated, discredited, politically bankrupt, and alone. Politically, they are yesterday's people. History has passed them by. Eastern Europe could never have achieved freedom by violent uprising. That would have incurred brutal repression and crushing defeat. Disciplined, non-violent action and peaceful people-power obtained what violence could never have achieved. The IRA may continue to kill. Their guns and explosives shall never persuade and therefore can never win.

SOCIALISM AND NATIONALISM

Another inner contradiction in the Sinn Féin/IRA movement lies in their failure to reconcile their commitment to socialism and their commitment to nationalism. Some republicans, commenting on the 1977 'Bodenstown Declaration' that republican aims could not be achieved by military means and that the IRA 'could not militarily defeat the British Army' concluded that 'the "military campaign" must be accompanied by a political struggle cum revolution' to the ends of 'achieving a political goal, namely a thirty-two county democratic socialist republic'.

Yet, they went on, the movement is still 'stuck' with 'giving primacy to the armed struggle', and presenting this to their putative supporters, in purely nationalist terms, as an effective means, and the only means, of 'getting the Brits out'. What happens 'after the end of the British presence' is a question which, they admit, is shelved as something which will be 'sorted out later' after 'Brits out'. It is admitted that the question of the definition of republican socialism, or of a policy and programme for a 'democratic socialist Irish republic', is barely debated among activists and is hardly even acknowledged before putative supporters, much less explained or admitted to them when votes are being sought.

This surely is at best an admission of political ineptitude, at worst a failure in political honesty. Even before the dramatic developments in Eastern Europe, the word 'socialism' had very little descriptive content left, being appropriated by so many vastly different leaders and regimes, irreconcilable with one another and often implacably hostile to one another. What was there in common between the socialisms of Joseph Stalin, Leonid Brezhnev, Nicolae Ceausescu, Enver Hoxha, Ho Chi Minh, Deng Xiaoping, Fidel Castro, Georges Marchais, François Mitterrand, not to speak of the socialism of Clement Attlee, Harold Wilson and Neil Kinnock? Socialism has become one of those words that has minimal and elusive descriptive content, accompanied with strong positive or negative emotive force. To call a movement 'socialist' is to tell us virtually nothing about its ideology, its principles, its aims, its strategies and its methods. It is inexcusable for a movement calling itself socialist to fail to clarify for itself and for the public the meaning it is giving to that term.

The failure and collapse of socialist regimes in Eastern Europe and the knowledge now available about the tyranny, the cruelty, the denial of human rights, the suppression of freedom, the mass murder and sometimes genocide practised by these regimes create a still more urgent duty and need for movements styling themselves socialist or even 'democratic socialist' to elucidate their definition of the term 'socialist'.

It is widely claimed nowadays that events in Eastern Europe have discredited and disvalued the very notion of socialism, or even that these events demonstrate the truth and the virtue of capitalism. Neither assumption is true. There is a place and indeed a need for socialism, if and in so far as this is understood as commitment to social justice, concern for fair shares for the weak, distributive justice for the disadvantaged, provision of all that constitutes a just and compassionate society. There could be a place in Irish political life for another socialist movement, in addition to the existing constitutional parties with socialist aims – a movement that honestly declared and explained its socialist name and aims, openly outlined realistic programmes for the economically viable achievement of those aims and stated a credible strategy for achieving them without incurring the spiritual, moral, financial and political bankruptcy of so many socialist regimes in Eastern Europe and elsewhere. There could be a place in Irish political life for a party that genuinely identified with the poor and oppressed and worked to ensure human rights and justice and equality for working-class housing estates and communities. There could be a place in Ireland for a reconstructed and non-violent Sinn Féin. But Sinn Féin will have no place and no future in Ireland unless and until it abandons violence and commits itself unequivocally to the non-violent democratic process.

The internal tension in Sinn Féin/IRA ideology, and the tension between each of these and the 'armed struggle' is illustrated by the glaring failure of the movement to achieve one of its central declared political and socialist aims, namely to unite 'workers, small farmers and small business people' in the proposed 'broad pan-nationalist alliance'. When workers, both Protestant and Catholic, are bombed or shot to death, when construction workers become legitimate targets, when working or unemployed families have their houses commandeered at gunpoint, their cars hijacked, perhaps members of their family forced by armed and hooded men to drive vans laden with IRA bombs, sometimes to the callously and ruthlessly intended self-destruction of the driver, when Protestant small farmers are systematically murdered, when small-business people have their premises bombed or robbed, or have protection money levied on their businesses, when workers have their places of employment wrecked and destroyed by bombs, the call for a united front of workers, farmers, and business people with Sinn Féin and the IRA becomes an insult to intelligence.

No alternative to peace

Northern Ireland is often said to be a place with two mutually irreconcilable visions of its identity and its future, the unionist one and the nationalist one. It would be more accurate to say that there are in Northern Ireland three different visions of its identity and its future, the unionist one, the constitutional nationalist one, and the militant republican one; and these are mutually irreconcilable with one another. The difference between the militant republican and the constitutional nationalist visions is not just a difference of methods to achieve the same agreed end; it is a difference of essence, a difference of fundamental moral principle, a difference of political analysis, a difference of political morality. The two visions radically diverge, not only in their respective attitudes to the use of violence, but also in their capacity or their willingness to recognise the reality and the legitimacy of the British/unionist presence in Ireland and the rights of the unionist community to be and to remain both unionist and British and to cling to the United Kingdom allegiance. The unionist vision differs from both the other visions in relation to its capacity or willingness to recognise the reality of the Irish/nationalist presence in Northern Ireland and the rights of the nationalist community to be and to remain Irish and cling to Irish identity and aspire to an eventual Irish unity.

The communities that espouse these visions can either choose to coexist in creative interaction with one another or condemn themselves to mutually destructive and self-destructive conflict with one another. The only way in which any of the respective aims can be brought to realisation in the longer term is the renunciation of violence and the restoration of peace. The indispensable condition of peace in the shorter term is that the special and unique political diversity that exists within the population of Northern Ireland be given appropriate institutional expression, providing equal constitutional legitimacy and full and unqualified constitutional recognition to the Irish identity and giving full political and civic rights to the Irish nationalist community within Northern Ireland, while at the same time giving full legitimacy and recognition to the unionist and British community within Northern Ireland. Neither of these communities is coterminous with the territory of Northern Ireland, but together they constitute the politico-demographic reality of Northern Ireland, and they have equally valid rights of legitimacy within a Northern Ireland with which each of these can identify.

When and only when these two rights are recognised and the appropriate institutional arrangements are peacefully accepted by both communities can the exponents of any of the three visions described have any hope of achieving their long-term aims. Given these conditions, unionists have every opportunity to persuade, and must believe in their capacity to persuade, nationalists in the longer run that their best future politically and economically lies in Northern Ireland, conceived constitutionally as part of the United Kingdom, but provided with those political and constitutional adjustments required to accommodate the unique and peculiar political and politico-national diversity of its population. Given these conditions, nationalists can have every opportunity to persuade, and can hope to be able to persuade, unionists that in the long term their best political and economic future lies in some agreed form of association with a united Ireland, in which the British and unionist identity is fully and permanently guaranteed for as long as unionists so demand, and their political, civil and religious rights are fully safeguarded, a united Ireland, therefore, endowed with the political and constitutional adjustments that are justly required in order to accommodate the religious, cultural, political and politico-national diversity that distinguishes the unionist from the nationalist population in the island of Ireland.

Given the conditions outlined, Sinn Féin has the opportunity to persuade, and can and must believe in its ability in the longer term to persuade, unionists and nationalists that the best hope for both lies in the long-term future in the republican vision of an Ireland that has finally achieved its aim of national independence and sovereignty in a democratic, Irish, socialist republic.

But the only condition on which Sinn Féin can have this opportunity, or can have any hope ever of persuading unionists and other nationalists to accept their vision of a future Ireland, is that the IRA cease their violence now. Once they cease their campaign of violence, they can work for that pan-nationalist consensus they have themselves admitted to be essential for achieving their objectives. They can then re-enter the democratic process and put their trust, as all democrats must do, in the truth and power of their own ideas and ideals. Unless and until they do abandon violence, they have no political present except irrelevance and no future except ignominious failure, and will leave no memory except one of shame.

For any of the political communities in Northern Ireland, there is no hope of advancing or even of sustaining their respective vision for Northern Ireland or for Ireland except through the restoration of peace. In a situation of peace, any of the futures could in the long term be open, any of the options becomes feasible. Political dialogue and the normal evolution of the democratic process will in time decide which option shall prevail and which future shall secure agreement and win consensus. For unionists as for nationalists as for republicans, everything is possible with peace. For republicans as much as for unionists and for nationalists there is no alternative to peace.

This in turn means that there is no alternative to dialogue. There is an urgent need and an imperative duty for everyone to repudiate violence and for all who repudiate violence to engage in talks about the future. Not to do so is to confess lack of confidence in the truth and the power of one's political convictions. Above all, it is tantamount to a tacit admission that the communities cannot agree between themselves as to how to share Northern Ireland with one another in peace and mutual respect and how to work constructively together for the welfare of all its citizens. That in turn could be read by paramilitaries as an admission that their blood-stained and tear-drenched way is the only way.

Pope Pius XII pleaded passionately for peace on the eve of the outbreak of World War Two. He declared: 'Nothing is lost by peace; everything may be lost by war' (*Acta Apostolica Sedis*, 11 September 1939, p. 334). I address a similar passionate plea to republican paramilitaries at this time.

185

# 9

## THE ECUMENICAL IMPERATIVE

*Let no one ever doubt the commitment of the Catholic Church
and the Apostolic See of Rome to the pursuit of the unity of
Christians . . . I renew that commitment and that pledge today
here in Ireland, where reconciliation between Christians takes
on a special urgency, but where it also has special resources in
the tradition of Christian faith and fidelity to religion which
marks both the Catholic and the Protestant communities . . .*

*Christians must unite together to promote justice and defend
the rights and dignity of every human person. All Christians
in Ireland must join together in opposing all violence and all
assaults against the human person – from whatever quarter
they come – and in finding Christian answers to the grave
problems of Northern Ireland. We must all be ministers of
reconciliation. We must by example as well as by word try to
move citizens, communities and politicians towards the ways
of tolerance, co-operation and love. No fear of criticism, no
risk of resentment, must deter us from this task. The charity of
Christ compels us. Precisely because we have a common Lord,
Jesus Christ, we must accept together the responsibility of the
vocation we have received from him.* [Pope John Paul II, Address to
the Ecumenical Meeting, Dublin, 29 September 1979; in *The Pope in
Ireland*, pp. 35–6]


RELIGIOUS WAR OR POLITICAL PROBLEM?

In their book *Integration and Division*, Frederick W. Boal and
J. Neville H. Douglas of the Department of Geography at
Queen's University Belfast, remark:

The strife . . . which has lasted since 1969 . . . is labelled as a
conflict between Protestants and Roman Catholics and has been
treated, in many instances, as a religious or holy war. Two
points must be made at the outset – first, that the Northern
Ireland problem pre-dates the existence of Northern Ireland as
a political unit, and secondly, that the holy war interpretation is,
at best, a vast over-simplification which enables its adherents to

189

avoid any attempt at real understanding. [Frederick W. Boal and J. Neville H. Douglas, *Integration and Division*, Academic Press, London, 1982, p. 1]

The communities polarised by the conflict in Northern Ireland are differentiated by history, culture, sense of historical origin and sense of national identity, political allegiance and political aspiration. They are differentiated by contrasting experience of social and economic opportunity, by their respective sense of power and powerlessness, of majority or of minority status. The communities are differentiated at the same time by religious or denominational background; and the other differences have historically been associated with the denominational differences. This is what gives the conflict the appearance of a religious war. This is what causes pain and even scandal to Christians everywhere. This is what constitutes in the eyes of many a serious difficulty for ecumenism. This is what creates a counter-witness to Christianity before the non-Christian religious world and a ready argument against religion in the hands of unbelievers.

Neither the religious nor the political analysis of the Northern Ireland problem should be developed to the exclusion of the other. Both aspects must be included in any adequate definition of our problem. Each explanation has been unilaterally developed by interested groups as part of a hand-washing exercise. I suggest that governments and politicians have sometimes developed the religious war model as an excuse for opting out of their political or governmental responsibilities. Equally, Churchmen have appealed to the political model as a means of opting out of their religious responsibilities as Churchmen. Politicians should be the last people to deny or to minimise the political elements in the conflict. Churchmen should be the last to deny its religious aspects.

Undeniably a religious dimension overlays all the other aspects; but the religious factor would not in itself produce conflict if the other factors were not allied with it. It is, however, also true that the non-religious factors take on a new character because of the religious dimension. I suggest that the religious dimension is very often a religion surrogate, a

190

secularised sediment of a former genuinely religious conviction. Secularised religion often retains the passionate conviction of religious belief long after the original religious belief has
been discarded. There are, for example, indubitably religious
features to be discerned in the supposedly irreligious ideology
of Marxism and indeed in some manifestations of dogmatic
secularism. A French religious sociologist once remarked that
France has become 'a pagan country with Christian supersti-
tions'. Some aspects of the Northern scene seem to invite a
similar comment. This is part of the challenge to the Churches
in Northern Ireland today.

WHEN RELIGION BECOMES IDEOLOGY

Even members of the respective communities can come to
perceive their struggle as religious as well as political. Extremists
in the loyalist community can believe that they are defending
Protestant values and the Protestant way of life against Roman
Catholic attack, because the membership of the IRA finds the
water in which it swims within the Roman Catholic population.
Paramilitaries in the loyalist community can claim to be defending Protestantism or Bible Christianity. This can be so
even when they have long ceased to practise any form of Christianity, have no connection with any Church, have never received any form of religious instruction and may in fact never
have been baptised. Their Protestantism is sociological, not
religious. Their Christianity is a politico-cultural ideology re-
sulting from a secularisation of the Protestantism whose religious
content they have abandoned.

Correspondingly, republican paramilitaries in the nationalist
community can claim to be defending the Catholic population
from the danger of sectarian attack from Protestant paramilitaries. In fact there is ground for suspicion that at times
IRA murders of Protestants have been intended to provoke
loyalist terrorist retaliation in order to create among Catholics
a felt need for IRA 'protection', in order thereby to keep the
water suitable for the IRA fish to swim in. IRA spokesmen will

protest that the Protestants they kill are 'legitimate targets' because they serve in the British security forces or because they support loyalist terrorism. They indignantly reject the charge of sectarian murder. But the protests are hollow. It is totally predictable and wholly inevitable that Protestants should perceive these killings to be sectarian murders of Protestants as Protestants and, especially along the border areas, as part of a campaign to intimidate and expel isolated Protestant inhabitants.

I said that loyalist extremists and paramilitaries represent a secularisation of Protestantism. Something corresponding can be said about republican paramilitaries. Religious traditions, I suggest, secularise in characteristically different ways. One characteristic way in which Irish Catholicism secularises is the way of revolutionary nationalist ideology. The Irish struggle for national independence was often presented in quasi-religious terms – terms of redemptive sacrifice and national resurrection. The Cause is presented still as something sacred, almost holy, whose 'patriot dead' have something of the halo of martyrdom and sainthood. Catholic religious images and symbols have been subtly used to give a quasi-religious aura to heroes of the 'armed struggle'. This was particularly true in the case of the graffiti that accompanied the tragic hunger strike of 1981 when the Gospel beatitudes were calculatedly misrepresented and the Christ figure and the Passion were deliberately misappropriated for political and paramilitary ends.

The fact that the Irish conflict is in part motivated by two opposing formerly religious ideologies points both to the paradoxical religious appearances of the struggle and to the impotence of the Churches alone to resolve it. Former Christians, Catholic or Protestant, may retain prejudices, passions and fanaticism of a pseudo-religious kind. Such people are totally and defiantly outside all influence from the living Church. They retain, alas, some of the rancours and resentments, suspicions and fears and hates inherited from the past. I must note that the replacement of religion by ideology need not be total; but, to speak of republican paramilitaries, over the whole range of argument and activity connected with 'the Cause', they have resolutely sealed off mind, heart and conscience from all influence by Catholic Church teaching and are systematically schooled in deafness to all appeals from clergy, bishops or Pope.

## PROTESTANT INSECURITY

The present situation in Northern Ireland is one of particular difficulty for the Churches, but also one of exceptional opportunity. At the present moment, for example, special difficulties are confronting the leaders of the Protestant Churches. This is no reason for complacency or for any propensity towards a feeling of superiority on the part of Catholics. Much less is it an occasion for self-satisfaction. This would be unworthy and un-Christian. Rather, this is a time for Catholics and especially for Catholic Churchmen to make genuine efforts to understand the problems faced by our Protestant brethren, to sympathise with their difficulties, and to support them in their Christian task of discernment and leadership.

The Catholic minority in the Northern Ireland state would traditionally have felt that Protestants were assured in their majority monopoly of power, property and privilege, and were secure in having their constitutional position irrevocably guaranteed by the British government. It can now be seen in retrospect that the assurance and confidence were only on the surface. They always concealed a deep and pervasive insecurity. The sense of being a threatened and besieged minority has always been strong among Northern Ireland Protestants. Professor Oliver MacDonagh has said of them:

> The siege of Derry in 1689 is their original and most powerful myth. They seem to see themselves in that, and since then, as an embattled and enduring people. Their historical self-vision is of an endless repetition of repelled assaults, without hope of absolute finality or fundamental change in their relationship to their surroundings and surrounded neighbours. [Quoted in Terence Brown, *The Whole Protestant Community: the making of an historical myth*, Field Day Pamphlet, no. 7, 1985, p. 8]

There is, of course, an objective basis in history and in fact for this sense of siege. Protestants are a minority in the island of Ireland. They fear that, even in Northern Ireland, the balance of population may in the longer term be changing, that their majority might gradually become threatened by a growth in the Catholic population. In the last twenty-one years, they have seen unionists' control of their own affairs gradually eroded and unionist institutions progressively dismantled. The ending of devolved government by direct rule, the loss of the potent political reality and powerfully reassuring symbolism represented by Stormont, the gradual loss of confidence by unionists in the British government's commitment to unionist interests, all of these have been factors for ever-increasing insecurity. Unionists have come to feel themselves misunderstood, unappreciated, unsupported and unwanted. They feel themselves abandoned to their own resources, isolated and without allies. All these factors combine to make unionists think of themselves as a threatened minority, without reliable friends and surrounded by real enemies. This mentality can very easily be inflamed by demagogic leaders and brought to dangerous emotional extremes.

The unionist sense of siege takes on religious overtones. The leaders who stress it most strongly seem to have a predilection for those Old Testament texts that speak of the Israelites as God's covenanted people, surrounded by enemies and needing to resist attack in every generation. The Israelites saw their history in religious terms. The Northern Ireland Protestant community have also been inclined to a 'sacral reading of history', with all the risk this carries with it of confusing their community's political interests with the cause of God (see Brown, p. 6, referring again to MacDonagh). Biblical terms, such as 'covenant', have often been invoked to describe unionist political campaigns. There were biblical overtones to the Ulster Covenant of 1912 and people gathered to sign it amid scenes of quasi-religious fervour. Some perfervid signatories signed it in their own blood.

It is recounted that in August 1971, at a time of great

community turbulence accompanying the introduction of internment, a handbill was circulated on the Newtownards Road in Belfast proclaiming, 'The enemies of our Faith and Freedom are determined to destroy the state of Northern Ireland and thereby enslave the people of God.' A newspaper advertisement in Belfast on Saturday 23 November 1985 bore the headline: 'Hearken Ulster: the Bible Answer to the Anglo-Irish Agreement'. After a series of quotations from the Old Testament, the text concluded: 'O People of Ulster, you are God's Israel ... God gave your forefathers this land, to be a light in darkest Ireland. These promises are yours. Pray daily for divine deliverance.' The unnamed group that placed the advertisement is probably an eccentric religious group, but the confusion of the political and the religious is a recurrent and continuing feature of the history of Ulster unionism.

The unionist/loyalist political rally held in the centre of Belfast on Saturday 23 November 1985 to protest against the Anglo-Irish Agreement began with the singing of the hymn 'O God, our help in ages past', and this was followed by a reading from Scripture. One of the platform spokesmen ended his speech with the words, 'May God defend the right'. The singing of religious hymns, the reading of Scripture lessons and the use of religious oratory on party political occasions and in support of party political positions are surely open to serious question on religious grounds. The continuing close connection between the unionist political parties and the Protestant religious or quasi-religious organisations, the Loyal Orange Order and the Royal Black Preceptory, is surely an anachronism and hard to justify in terms of open, democratic politics. It is a feature of Ulster unionist history that from generation to generation a series of messianic-type leaders have emerged, in the guise of the biblical prophets, to recall 'the Protestant people' to biblical orthodoxy and political purity. For such leaders, religious orthodoxy and political purity are identical. As the Revd John Morrow has pointed out, 'political and theological betrayal go hand in hand' (John Morrow, 'Ecumenism in Ireland' in James McLoone [ed.], *Being Protestant in Ireland,* Co-operation North in association with the Social Study Conference, 1984, p. 51). Professor Austin Fulton suggested that theological development was sometimes influenced by politics, and that theological attitudes could be welcomed or rejected 'accordingly as they are thought to strengthen or to weaken strongly-held political positions' (quoted in Brown, p. 16). Political convictions can come to be held with a quasi-religious fervour, and regarded as moral absolutes beyond the reach of time or change.

The danger to religion in all this is obvious. When religious beliefs are identified with political positions we have the beginning of the relativising of religion, which really is the substitution of religion by secularism, or the replacement of the true God by political and secular idols. The first biblical Commandment is:

> The Lord your God is one Lord
> You shall have no God except me.
> [Exodus 20: 2–3]

God alone is absolute, everything else is relative. To regard political beliefs as absolute is to absolutise the relative, and this is equivalently to relativise the absolute, and to substitute what is not God for God. It is a form of idolatory. It is particularly repugnant to the true genius of Protestantism.

## REPUBLICAN IDEOLOGY

There are curious similarities between this view of politics, held by some Protestants, and the pseudo-mystical republican view espoused by some Catholics. The Anglican Archbishop of Dublin, Dr Donald Caird, some years ago spoke of the blend of 'political nationalism and physical force, allied with religious mysticism', in the republican movement (Donald A.R. Caird, 'Protestantism and national identity', in McLoone [ed.], p. 59). Just as loyalism/unionism can be a secularised version of Protestantism, so republicanism/nationalism can be a secularised version of Catholicism. A parallel danger of idolatry can be latent in both. For physical force republicans, the Nation, the Cause, the Rising are erected into absolutes, demanding the total commitment and unqualified obedience that only God can truly ask. The Nation and the Cause become self-justifying sources of moral value, superseding the Ten Commandments whenever these stand in the way of 'the armed struggle'. Moral absolutes are relativised. Right becomes what the struggle requires. The Cause can turn wrong into right. The end justifies every means. The political community becomes in a sense the true 'people of God': and the Church is relativised into a human institution, a part of the Establishment, its teaching judged and found wanting by the standards of another gospel, the gospel of the Republic.

Happily, this pseudo-mystical nationalism is now a much less potent force in the Republic than it has been for eighty years. It is decidedly a minority view among nationalists in Northern Ireland. Nevertheless, it is important that Catholics recognise it for what it is and appreciate the dangers it poses for our Catholic faith and morality.

FEAR OF THE CHURCH OF ROME

There is in Northern Ireland Protestantism a deep-seated fear and suspicion of the Church of Rome. Much of this fear is based on ignorance of Catholic doctrines and practices, and could be alleviated by better religious education among Protestants and by increased Protestant–Catholic contacts and dialogue. The persistent anti-Roman element in much popular Protestantism is an important factor in community conflict in the North. The Catholic Church must pay serious attention to it and earnestly seek ways in which it might be lessened and eventually removed. Catholic bishops, clergy and laity must be particularly sensitive to this problem, and must do everything possible, in their words and by their lives, to witness to the true nature and authentic teaching of the Catholic Church.

Catholics must seek to understand the historical roots of the fears and suspicions of Protestants. We must try honestly to acknowledge the faults in ourselves that foster Protestant misunderstandings and prejudices. The roots of fear and suspicion may lie in the past, but their continuance in the present must be in some measure due to what we Catholics have done or have failed to do in our understanding of our own Catholic faith and in our living of it and witnessing to it. It might be presumptuous of me to claim to speak to Protestants, but I would dearly love to say to them, in the name of the Catholic community, that we Catholics have no designs towards Protestants other than respect for their faith and their Christian moral witness, and eagerness to profit from the spiritual riches of the Protestant tradition. I was myself brought up in my youth to respect Protestants' moral uprightness, industry, efficiency, honesty and good neighbourliness. 'A Protestant look about a place' was a compliment and a matter for emulation in the north Antrim of my boyhood. We Catholics desire nothing more than to share this land with Protestants, not just in cool and distant coexistence but in Christian brotherhood and sisterhood under the Fatherhood of the God whom we both call Our Father, and under the lordship of Christ, whom we both acclaim as our common Lord.

Anti-Catholic prejudice is not, however, a problem to be solved by Catholics alone. The existence and the persistence of this prejudice is a problem also for the Protestant Churches. They have a Christian responsibility to seek to become more accurately informed about the Catholic Church, its self-understanding, its teaching, its beliefs, its worship and its practices, and to help their members to 'represent the condition [of Catholics] with truth and fairness' (*Unitatis Redintegratio*, no. 5), so that Churches may be able to speak the truth about one another and to one another in love, and that the disagreements that persist may at least be based upon accurate understanding.

Much mutual religious suspicion and prejudice is due to religious ignorance. This ignorance is twofold. It often is ignorance of the teaching of our own Church, leading to lack of full acceptance of the internal renewal in which each of our Churches has been engaged over recent decades. There is also ignorance of and therefore opposition to the ecumenical movement. It is worth remarking that the modern ecumenical movement began in the Protestant Churches; but the movement has been entered with enthusiasm by the Catholic Church, particularly since the Vatican Council. There is still great need for ecumenical education and for acceptance of ecumenism, not as a betrayal or as a threat, but as an opportunity for new understanding of our own truth and for the enrichment of our own religious tradition through contact with others.

A RECONCILING CHURCH

The Church is called to be itself a prototype of a just and reconciled society. We cannot be credible to the world unless we live reconciliation ourselves as well as preaching it. St Augustine spoke of the Church as that part of the world that has already been reconciled. The Church, he said, is 'the reconciled world' (Sermon 96: 7–8). Pope Paul VI commented on this saying of Augustine as follows:

> The duty of making peace extends personally to each and every member of the faithful. If it is not fulfilled, even the sacrifice of worship which they intend to offer (Matthew 5: 23 ff.) remains ineffective. Mutual reconciliation, in fact, shares in the very value of the sacrifice itself, and together with it constitutes a single offering pleasing to God . . .
>
> The church therefore, because she is 'a reconciled world', is also a reality that is by nature permanently reconciling. As such she is the presence and the action of God, who 'in Christ was reconciling the world to Himself' (2 Corinthians 5: 19). This action and presence are expressed primarily in Baptism, in the forgiveness of sins and in the Eucharistic celebration, which is the renewal of the redeeming sacrifice of Christ and the effective sign of the unity of the People of God. [*De Reconciliatione in Ecclesia*, 1974]

Ecumenism is not an optional extra for Christians. It is at the heart of our faith. In the present circumstances, it has become a more urgent imperative than ever for us all.

All the Churches need a more vigorous campaign of adult religious education and of spiritual renewal. The closer becomes our relationship with Christ Our Saviour, and the deeper our commitment to our own Church, the greater will be our respect for other believers in Jesus Christ who is their Lord as well as ours.

Each Church community must seek and must help its members to seek an authentic understanding of the doctrines and traditions of the other Church communities. We all have inherited stereotyped and often caricatural ideas about one another's faith. The teaching we received may have been designed to refute the doctrines of others rather than to understand them. We may have learned about the points on which our faith differs from the faith of other communions, more than about the deep agreement or convergence there is between their faith and ours. We may have learned to feel religiously superior to others rather than to see how we can find inspiration and support for our own Christian faith in their beliefs and lives and witness.

In our pastoral practice, we Catholic bishops and priests have, I fear, not always given ecumenism the priority our Church assigns to it, a priority affirmed in the documents of the Second Vatican Council and in many post-conciliar documents and statements from the Popes and the Roman Congregations. The Vatican Council in its *Decree on Ecumenism* stressed that:

> The concern for restoring unity involves the whole Church, faithful and clergy alike. It extends to everyone, according to the talent of each, whether it be exercised in daily Christian living or in theological and historical studies. [*Unitatis Redintegratio*, no. 5]

The Council calls on us Catholics to make

> every effort to avoid expressions, judgements and actions which do not represent the condition of our separated brethren with truth and fairness, and so make mutual relations with them more difficult. [*Ibid.*, no. 4]

The Council asks Catholics

> gladly [to] acknowledge and esteem the truly Christian endowments for our common heritage which are to be found among our separated brethren. It is right and salutary to recognise the

riches of Christ and virtuous works in the lives of others who
are bearing witness to Christ, sometimes even to the shedding
of their blood. God is always wonderful in his works and worthy
of all praise. Nor should we forget that anything wrought by the
grace of the Holy Spirit in the hearts of our separated brethren
can contribute to our own edification. [*Ibid.*, no. 4]

The Council stressed the close links between ecumenism
and Church renewal or reform, and between both and the
Church's mission to 'those who are far off'. It is a scandal to
many people overseas and many at home that in a society
where religious practice in all communions is so high, the
Churches have seemed so helpless in face of violence and enmity
and conflict between communities both claiming to be Christian.
This is not, of course, the whole story. I am firmly convinced
that, had it not been for the influence of the Churches and for
the preaching of the Gospel of love and reconciliation and
peace in all our Churches, and for the prayers offered for peace
in all Christian communions, the situation would have been
incomparably worse. Nevertheless, the Church's mission overseas, even her mission to those distanced from the Church at
home, is damaged by our failures and our omissions in the area
of ecumenism, or at least by our failing to give sustained priority
to ecumenism in our preaching and teaching and in our pastoral
work. We are called to repentance and conversion in this regard.

REPENTANCE

In so far as we in each of our Churches have failed to witness
to Christ's love in our attitudes to one another, in our language
about one another, in our readiness to respect one another's
convictions, to accept one another in our differences, to stand
up for one another's rights, we must ask God humbly for the
spirit of repentance and we must beg forgiveness from God
and from one another. For much that we have done and much
that we have failed to do we must repent. Above all, we must
amend our lives. Instead of covering our eyes and faces with
the cloak of self-righteousness like the Jews of old who cried,

'This is the Temple of the Lord; this is the Temple of the Lord', we must rather listen to the prophet, Jeremiah, warning us, 'But if you do amend your behaviour and your actions, if you do treat each other fairly . . . then here in this place I will stay with you' (Jeremiah 7: 5–7). I believe that practical steps can be taken to multiply opportunities for contact, for praying together, talking and listening together, sharing together, studying together, working and serving together. I shall suggest a few. Others may have different or better suggestions. But there should be no excuse for any of us for standing still where we are. We cannot refuse to hear 'what the Spirit is saying to the Churches' (Revelation 3: 22).

### PRAYER FOR CHRISTIAN UNITY

Prayer is the source of energy for all Christian movement and mission and ministry. The Vatican Council said in its *Decree on Ecumenism*:

> Change of heart and holiness of life, along with public and private prayer for the unity of Christians, should be regarded as the soul of the whole ecumenical movement, and can rightly be called 'spiritual ecumenism'. [*Unitatis Redintegratio*, no. 7]

Father Congar, in a moving description of the emotion he felt on the historic occasion of the meeting between Pope Paul VI and Patriarch Athenagoras in Jerusalem in 1963, remarks that he recalled at that moment his own mother, who had prayed faithfully throughout a long life for reunion between Christians. He recalled the prayers of other unknown Christian men and women throughout the ages and across the continents. He reflected that the historic meeting he was then witnessing was God's answer to the hidden prayers of these unknown praying instruments of Christian unity.

We all must pray regularly for unity between Christians. We should pray regularly for our Christian brothers and sisters of other communions, both in our public worship and in our family, group and personal prayer. It would surely be appropriate that worshippers in Catholic and Protestant churches in the same neighbourhood should frequently pray for one another's spiritual and material welfare, whether in the litanies or inter- cessions or prayers of the faithful, according to our respective liturgical traditions. It can be more meaningful to pray for the Protestant or Catholic Christians in the next church or churches down the road than simply to pray for Catholics or Protestants in general.

ECUMENICAL SERVICES

Ecumenical services are now a familiar feature of the Week of Prayer for Christian Unity. We must not allow this kind of meeting for prayer to be confined to a one-off annual flurry of activity, engaged in for one week during the year and celebrated in a few familiar centres recognised for ecumenical celebrations. We must not forget that there are many areas of Belfast and of Northern Ireland which are totally unfamiliar with such joint meetings for prayer and even, in the case of some Protestant communities, staunchly opposed to such meetings. We must earnestly try to extend these services to new areas and to en- courage new congregations and new groups to participate in them.

I believe that, in addition to the familiar centres for ecu- menical worship, we should now be trying to develop inter- congregational contacts between parishes and congregations throughout our Churches, so as to involve more and more of our so-called ordinary churchgoers in ecumenical activity. Neighbourhood churches should establish ongoing contacts with one another not just at the level of clergy and lay leaders but also at the level of the ordinary laity. This happens already in a number of areas, where different churches of different denomi- nations act in turn as hosts for ecumenical services and together arrange preachers from different traditions to address them.

These occasions must not be confined to one week of the year. They should be extended to other weeks throughout the year. The great central feasts of the year common to all Chris- tians are particularly suitable for witnessing in shared prayer to what we believe in common about the great 'mystery of God's purpose, the hidden plan He so kindly made in Christ from the beginning . . . that He would bring together everything under Christ as Head, everything in heaven and everything in earth' (Ephesians 1: 9–10).

Joint carol services at Christmas are one example. Their spiritual impact can be increased by the preparation of a linking biblical script, which helps the service to be a biblical prayerful reflection on the mystery of the Word made flesh. Easter is another privileged time for joint Christian witness to the definitive victory over sin and evil won for all of us by the resurrection of Christ from the dead. Pentecost is another special time for joint prayerful reflection on our call to seek for unity in Christ, under the influence of the one Spirit who enables all of us to say 'Jesus is Lord'.

There are occasions characteristic of our different traditions when sharing in prayer would also be appropriate and when we could mutually support our brethren in other communions at times which are spiritually significant for them. I think of Harvest Thanksgiving in some Protestant Churches or of the World Day of Prayer for Peace observed by Catholics annually on New Year's Day.

There are characteristic modes of prayer, experiences of prayer and theologies of prayer and outstanding spiritual and mystical writings in our different traditions, and it is spiritually enriching for all when these are shared among people of different traditions.

JOINT BIBLE READING

Much spiritual benefit, as well as growth in ecumenical understanding, can be derived from joint meetings for prayerful reading of Scripture and reflection and sharing on scriptural themes. Such meetings have often taken place under the auspices of the charismatic renewal movement. With sound theological direction and with care to preserve close relationships with the respective Churches, this movement has done much to promote among many Christians greater love of Scripture and lived application of scriptural teaching to daily experience. It has thereby made a significant contribution to ecumenism.

Some years ago, the Churches in Ireland organised a programme of joint distribution of the Gospels by members of all our Churches with the title, *Good News for Ireland.* I believe that a repetition of that experiment could be timely now. All of us derive our faith from the Bible. All of us are concerned about the sad ignorance of the Bible in much of modern society, and we are all convinced that only the Gospel message can bring hope to our despair and light in our darkness.

## CLERGY FRATERNALS

All of these activities require contact and co-operation between Protestant and Catholic clergy at local level. Such meetings happily are already a regular occurrence in many areas. In them, clergy meet on a regular basis for prayer, Bible study and pastoral discussion. I earnestly hope that clergy of all denominations may be willing to participate in such meetings. Church leaders must give the necessary encouragement and support. So many of our problems, pastoral and spiritual, as well as material, are common to the members of all our Churches. Social and economic problems such as poverty, unemployment, vandalism, youth alienation, and marriage breakdown are common to the members of all our Churches, and the exchange of ideas and experiences regarding them could not but be mutually beneficial. An important witness to Christian love can be given to our people in all communions by the spectacle of our clergy meeting openly together in friendship. The better we clergy come to know each other, the more we can hope to come to trust each other. Many of our community tensions come from lack of friendly contact and from lack of mutual trust.

## CHURCHES' ECUMENICAL FORUM

In order that ecumenical contacts might become more integrated into the ongoing practice of clergy and laity, some kind of informal committee representing the different Churches should be established at diocesan, presbytery or district level. Such a committee could monitor ecumenical activity and try to ensure its continuing momentum throughout the year. It could assess proposals for new initiatives and discuss practical difficulties and misunderstandings as they arise. At moments of inter-community tension or crisis, meetings of such a group could help to lessen tension or dissipate misunderstanding.

In my view, such a group should be informal and local, rather than nationwide. It would be better to avoid titles such as Council of Churches that could excessively institutionalise such a body and give a misleading idea of its scope and purpose. Simply for consideration, I propose such a title as Belfast Forum of Churches, the title obviously varying according to where each centre is set up. Each group could begin quietly and modestly and experimentally, and its usefulness could be assessed in the light of experience.

REGIONALISED ECUMENISM

A forum like this could liaise with what has come to be called the 'Ballymascanlon process'. Under the general umbrella of the Ballymascanlon Conference, regional mini-conferences have been organised in different parts of Ireland. I believe that a number of local mini-conferences of this kind should be held in the major centres here in the North, where the need for ecumenical activity is obviously greater.

THEOLOGICAL DIALOGUE

Theological dialogue is by no means the whole of ecumenism, but it is an indispensable element of it. Whilst the basic doctrine of the respective Churches is the same across Ireland and indeed across the world, specific nuances and special doctrinal emphases and preconceptions – as well as stereotyped reciprocal attitudes – characterise inherited inter-Church relationships here in the North as a result of history and culture and the overlap between religion and politics. There is a need for dialogue at regional level between competent and representative theologians from the different traditions in order to achieve more accurate understanding of the respective Church doctrines and practices. This more accurate understanding could then be transmitted to the main body of clergy and laity.

## SEMINARIANS AND CANDIDATES FOR THE MINISTRY

Ecumenism must be an important element in the theological and pastoral education and training of all candidates for the ministry. Catholic seminarians and Protestant candidates for the ordained ministry should have opportunities for joint contact and discussion and even, where possible, shared sessions or seminars. Catholic theologians could address Protestant students for the ministry and Protestant theologians could address Catholic students, so that mutual understanding and appreciation of different theological traditions may grow. Opportunities could thus be provided for Protestant and Catholic candidates for the ministry to form relationships in their student days, which could be the basis for continuing friendship and fellowship in ministry after ordination.

## ECUMENISM IN EDUCATION

Whilst deeply convinced of the value and the necessity of a Church-related system of education, and whilst therefore totally committed to the support of Catholic schools, I am also acutely aware of the obligation to develop ecumenical understanding and inter-community reconciliation through education. Indeed, any authentic programme of Catholic religious education must have a systematic ecumenical component. I therefore welcome the commitment of the present Minister for Education, Dr Brian Mawhinney, to the promotion and facilitation of Education for Mutual Understanding, and I am glad to say that this movement is being strongly supported throughout the Catholic school system. I welcome also the inclusion of cross-curricular themes in education programmes, including mutual understanding and heritage. I support the government commitment to the belief that 'the curriculum of every child should include elements of education for Mutual Understanding, which has already helped to foster valuable cross-community contacts among many of our schools'. I believe, however, that teachers, who are already over-burdened and over-pressurised, should be given all the additional staffing and facilities, resources and supports that are necessary if they are to work effectively in this area. This is essential because at the same time they have to carry the responsibility for a new extended curriculum and face the added strains of repeated, published assessment reports and the pressure from parents and public for good results.

Every encouragement should be given in all our Churches to the development of contacts between teachers and pupils in Catholic schools and their Protestant counterparts. There should be as much inter-school co-operation as possible in research projects, field trips, athletics. Teachers and pupils of both traditions should study sensitive topics such as Irish history, the history of the Christian Churches, Reformation and post-Reformation history. Clergy and teachers of one tradition should be invited to visit schools of the other tradition in order to share elements of our diverse cultural traditions and heritage with one another, and thereby be helped to form less enclosed and exclusive views about history and culture and identity in our native land.

The inter-Church report, entitled *Violence in Ireland*, presented to the Churches in 1976 called for 'a programme to combat sectarianism wherever it is found'. It defined sectarianism as 'the frame of mind that exploits denominational differences to promote a sense of superiority, a denial of rights, a justification of conflict' (*Violence in Ireland*, pp. 71–2). That programme is still urgently needed. I believe that sectarian attitudes are fostered by the historical identification of the Churches with political parties. The complete withdrawal from party politics of ministers of religion would be good both for religion and for politics.

THE MEDIA

The media play an important part in the furtherance of

208

ecumenical understanding. The first experience of Catholic–Protestant dialogue that many clergy in Northern Ireland had was through the religious advisory committees of the BBC or UTV. The broadcasting of church services gave many in the general public their first experience of worship in the other tradition, Catholic or Protestant as the case might be. This helped us to see what is common as well as better to understand the differences. Leading figures and clergy in other Churches have become familiar voices or faces. Newspaper coverage of religious events here in Northern Ireland is on the whole fair and balanced. Church co-operation with the media is an important element in spreading the Gospel message in the modern world. Talking on radio and television has helped many clergy to make the content and style of their sermons better adapted to modern congregations and more relevant to contemporary needs.

The role the media have played in the religious sphere will be put under growing pressure as newspapers, radio and television pass increasingly under monopolistic commercial ownership and become more and more subject to the demand for profits and dividends. The Churches should together use their influence to resist the pressures to squeeze out religious programmes or turn them into current affairs chat shows. Religious programming must not be made the prime casualty of budgetary cutbacks. I am confident that there are people in the media who will lend support to that plea.

SHARED SOCIAL CONCERN

Witness and work for justice and care for the poor and suffering are an important part of what the Spirit is saying to the Churches in our time. The longest section in the Vatican Council's *Decree on Ecumenism* (*Unitatis Redintegratio*, 21 November 1964) is that devoted to inter-Church co-operation in social matters and especially in efforts to 'relieve the afflictions of our times'. This co-operation is particularly relevant for our situation because of the economic difficulties in which we now find ourselves in both parts of Ireland. Members of all denominations are now affected, to greater or lesser degree, by unemployment, by redundancies and threats of redundancy, by environmental decay, particularly in urban areas, by homelessness. There is a challenge here to joint Christian action between the clergy and laity of all Churches. Much is being done by the Churches separately in trying to cope with these multiple problems of deprivation. Wherever it is possible, projects of this kind could be promoted on an inter-Church basis. This would be of benefit for ecumenical understanding and it would also be a witness of the caring Church before the whole community.

Care for the aged, the physically and mentally handicapped, the sick and the dying, and care for prisoners, is the Christian duty of us all. Happily, hospital chaplains have developed excellent ecumenical relationships and support one another in their work and witness. A similar situation exists in relation to prison chaplaincies. The hospice movement is an excellent example of this kind of caring. All such developments are enabling the Churches to be seen more manifestly in their true posture of common witness to love for society's 'little ones' and forgotten or rejected people.

In regard to marriage instability, we all face similar and growing problems. Experience and insights could usefully be exchanged between us in this domain. Inter-Church marriages can have special problems and need specific pastoral support. Joint pastoral care by the respective clergy can make a valuable contribution to the Christian living of such marriages and to the witness which at their best such marriages can make to inter-Church reconciliation.

OPTION FOR THE POOR

Deprivation is the lot of many in our society. It causes the same outrage to the human and Christian dignity of persons, whether they be Catholic or Protestant. The continuance and indeed the steady widening of the gap between rich and poor is a matter for concern to all Christians. The existence of poverty and deprivation is a reproach to the Christian professions of our society and of all our Churches. Complacency and inaction by the Church in the face of deprivation would lead the deprived and especially the young deprived into growing alienation from all religion. Deprivation, as I have argued in chapter 6, is closely linked with the origin and continuance of paramilitary violence. I am convinced that the credibility and the relevance of the Christian Churches in Ireland in these closing decades of the twentieth century will be judged predominantly by the criterion of our Christian response to the challenge of poverty and deprivation, and to the related challenge of paramilitary violence.

American generosity expressed through the International Fund for Ireland and through many other channels has significantly helped and can continue to help to alleviate the deprivation that feeds violence, which in turn increases deprivation. US business could, by industrial investment, help to create employment, and this would have a direct bearing upon the elimination of political violence, for people, and particularly young people, if left chronically unemployed and alienated, can be more readily recruited into paramilitary organisations. American Church generosity has helped and can continue to help to promote projects of genuine reconciliation in justice and respect for human rights between Protestants and Catholics, between republicans and unionists. Our American friends could help us to build an Ireland resembling that land of religious liberty, equality and tolerance under God that both Catholic Irishmen and Protestant Irishmen served so nobly to create in the United States, the land of their adoption, where both found freedom from coercion.

REJECTION OF VIOLENCE

There must be no reservation or equivocation or onesidedness about the Christian condemnation of all violence, whether to promote change of political institutions or to prevent such change. Churchmen must fearlessly and unitedly condemn all

211

physical violence, all verbal violence, and all the equivocation that suggests that violence, however 'regrettable', is in certain circumstances inevitable or understandable. There are no circumstances in Northern Ireland today in which resort to violence is or could be justified, whether to advance republican aims or to defend unionist aims. The condemnation of violence by the Churches must be clear, absolute and total.

I believe that Catholic Churchmen and Catholic spokespersons generally should be among the most prominent and persistent advocates of the rights of Protestants and should be first to condemn murders and outrages perpetrated against Protestants or threats to Protestants' rights. I believe equally that Protestant Churchmen and Protestant spokespersons generally should be among the most prominent and persistent advocates of the rights of Catholics and should be first to voice condemnation of injustices done to Catholics and to plead for Catholics' rights.

This is the prophetic voice required of the Church in Ireland in our time. It will call for courage from us all. We must not expect praise or popularity from some of 'our own people' in doing so. But it would be craven for us to prefer popularity to prophecy or to pursue expediency instead of truth and justice.

PEACE THROUGH THE CROSS

These ways forward are going to be for all of us ways of the Cross. Like Our Master, we can expect to be 'despised and rejected by men'. But, to use words chosen by Professor Jürgen Moltmann as titles for two of his works, the God we believe in is The Crucified God and that is why the Church we believe in is The Church in the Power of the Spirit.

Moltmann ends his book *The Church in the Power of the Spirit* with the words:

> The Church is apostolic when it takes up its cross. It then witnesses to the glory of the Risen Christ in its fellowship with those who suffer, and his future in its fellowship with the imprisoned. In our Godless and inhuman world 'the Church

212

under the Cross' shows itself to be the true apostolic Church. Its apostolic succession is the succession of the passion of Christ ... Unity in freedom, holiness in poverty, catholicity in partisan support for the weak, and apostolate in suffering, are the marks by which it is known in the world. [*The Church in the Power of the Spirit*, SCM Press, 1977, p. 361]

A great mass of suffering and sorrow has been borne by Protestants and Catholics in Northern Ireland over twenty-one blood-stained and tear-drenched years. May that suffering be an incentive for conversion, a source of hope, a strength for courage to face the future. The suffering that Irish Protestants and Catholics have endured can be a crucible for reconciliation between the two communities. I venture to quote something I have written in the past:

Our suffering can be redemptive. It can be reconciliatory. But it will be so only to the extent that we 'suffer with' each other as if the other's suffering were our own. 'Suffer with' is the strong, original meaning of the word 'sympathise'. Catholics must, in this strong sense, sympathise with Protestant sufferings, fears, insecurities; Protestants must sympathise with Catholic insecurities, fears, sufferings. That is how we 'complete in our flesh all that has still to be undergone by Christ' for the sake of all our Churches. [*Peace, the Work of Justice, Addresses on the Northern Tragedy, 1973–79*, Veritas Publications, Dublin, 1979, p. 35]

With Jesus Our Lord and Master we must every day 'resolutely take the road to Jerusalem' (Luke 9: 51). For us, as for Jesus, it will inevitably be a Via Dolorosa; but it is also the way of salvation for ourselves and the Church, the way to glory for each of us and for our Churches, in Christ Jesus with the Father. Let our prayer be:

Glory be to Him whose power working in us can do infinitely more than we can ask or imagine. Glory be to Him, from generation to generation in the Church and in Christ Jesus for ever and ever. Amen. [Ephesians 3: 20–1]

# 10
## PEACE AND YOUTH

*I appeal to young people who may have become caught up in
organisations engaged in violence. I say to you, with all the
love, all the respect, with all the trust I have in young people:
Do not listen to voices that speak the language of hatred,
revenge, retaliation. Do not follow any leaders who train you
in the ways of inflicting death. Love life, respect life; in yourselves and in others. Give yourselves to the service of life, not
the work of death.* [Pope John Paul II, Address at Drogheda, 29 September 1979; in *The Pope in Ireland*, p. 23]

In his New Year's message for 1985, the International Year of
Youth, Pope John Paul II emphasised how the desire for peace
arises spontaneously from the hearts of the youth of the world,
and how peace needs the commitment, energy and enthusiasm
of youth if it is to triumph over hatred, violence, oppression
and injustice.

Since 1969 our country has been plagued by violence. There
has been set up a vicious spiral of violence, in which we are now
tragically entangled. Young people have to decide where they
stand in relation to this violence. Whether society is to sink
deeper into the nihilistic and despairing cult of violence, or opts
instead for the positive task of constructing peace non-violently,
depends largely on the fundamental moral choices a new generation of men and women are being called upon to make.

FUNDAMENTAL MORAL CHOICES

Young people today are sensitive, even more than were earlier
generations, to the demands of justice and to the sanctity of
human rights. The most fundamental of all human rights is the
right to life. The most basic of all moral principles is absolute
respect for human life. Justice in society depends upon respecting the right to life of others, even when they differ from us
politically, ideologically or otherwise.

Justice in society depends upon acceptance of a moral order to which society must conform. Justice implies that right must prevail over might and that moral right be clearly distinguished from moral wrong. Right is not what the men with money and power or the men with guns and bombs say is right, but what conscience, based on objective moral values, pronounces right. Conscience must be determined by how things morally are in themselves. What is morally good is good, no matter what public opinion or opinion polls may say. What is morally wrong is wrong, no matter what organisation says it is right, no matter how many may be claimed to vote for it, no matter what leader orders it to be done.

Our moral choices are our own personal and eternal responsibility. We can never excuse them by appealing to 'the Cause', or 'the Movement', or 'the War', or 'higher orders'. We cannot surrender our conscience to any cause or any organisation or any leader. St Thomas More, martyr of conscience against despotism, said, 'I will not pin my conscience on to any man's back.'

To young people who may have become involved in paramilitary organisations, I would like to say: you must obey God rather than men. When God says, 'Thou shalt not kill', you cannot plead the excuse that someone ordered you to do it, or that 'the War' or 'the Revolution' required it.

To do this is to put the Cause or the Revolution in the place of God. It is to place false gods before the true and living God. Let young people today face the vital question: Who is your God? Is it the true and living God revealed to us by Jesus Christ; or is it some spurious substitute for God? To claim that the end justifies the means, that a good end makes evil means good, that 'anything is permissible and right in war', is the end of all morality. This is precisely what every militaristic imperialism in past or recent history has claimed. This is exactly what every totalitarian and oppressive regime maintains. This is the philosophy of unbridled capitalism, a recent exponent of which is quoted as saying, 'Business is war', thereby implying that all means are good which make a profit. This is the philosophy of right-wing 'national security' regimes in military dictatorships and police states the world over. This is the philosophy of left-wing Marxist–Leninist regimes wherever they have been able to establish their control.

## SOCIAL DESTRUCTIVENESS OF VIOLENCE

Those who live in areas marked by political violence are best placed to appreciate its awful human cost and waste. Today's teenagers and young adults can best recognise the ugly face behind the mask of romantic rhetoric. The republican physical force campaign has dragged on since 1969, and is no whit nearer to achieving any of its political objectives. To be talking of 'a long war' after so many years of misery is surely an admission that the struggle has led nowhere and is leading nowhere.

Meanwhile, the nationalist community is itself the first and chief victim of the physical force campaign. The economic and environmental misery of deprived nationalist areas has been aggravated by this campaign. The breakdown of law and order, the scourge of criminal vandalism, the extortion of protection money, the proliferation of political drinking clubs are an inevitable offshoot of this campaign. Violence oppresses the oppressed instead of liberating them.

A whole population is being held to ransom and made to suffer as a result of a mythology of revolution. A whole generation of young people is having its young lives blighted by it. Nationalist communities should ask themselves how much longer they are prepared to be sacrificial victims to a Moloch-like idol of revolution.

Of all the ways available to the nationalist community to achieve justice, violence is the one way that is doomed to fail. As Pope Paul VI said in his stirring encyclical on world justice, *Populorum Progressio*, 'A present evil should not be fought at the cost of greater misery' (*Populorum Progressio*, 1967, paragraph 31).

## JUSTICE THROUGH NON-VIOLENCE

Some will say that if the physical force movement were called off, the Irish nationalist cause would be abandoned and nationalists would be left without hope of justice. This is absolutely not true. The truth is that, if physical force were renounced, a powerful movement of moral force could be generated by a united nationalist community, which would merit strong international sympathy and support and would prevail. All over the world, moral force and not physical force is the strength of the oppressed. Only moral force brings true liberation. The physical force movement in Ireland today is undermining the moral force of the nationalist struggle for justice. It is dividing the nationalist community. It is obscuring the moral issues. It is creating a climate for repression of nationalist communities by the security forces. It is invoked by spokesmen for the unionist community as their justification for intransigence. It makes the struggle for justice immeasurably more difficult. The struggle for justice can really succeed only when the guns and the bombs are silenced.

## Through non-violence to justice and peace

In 1977, in the heart of strife-torn Derry, Archbishop Helder Camara of Brazil was asked, 'Is there a non-violent way to change unjust structures?' He replied, 'My answer and my deep conviction is: Yes.' He instanced Mahatma Gandhi and Martin Luther King as heroes of non-violence, who were put to death precisely because their non-violent leadership presented a greater threat to those exerting institutional violence than guns or bombs. We can add the heroic Lech Walesa to the roll of honour of the non-violent. In a homily during the visit to Ireland, Helder Camara said:

> Non-violence is in the long run strong. Violence is weak. Crushing injustices do exist; but there are growing up everywhere groups of people working to change the structures of society. And we will win. We will win because Christ is with us. God is a living God, who hears the voice of His people. It is impossible that, in a world created by the Father who is love, liberated by the Son who is love, and filled with the Holy Spirit who is love,

220

it is impossible that the last word can be the 'No' of death and despair.

Pope John Paul II says to young people:

> Whatever paths you set out upon, do so with hope and trust: hope in the future that, with God's help, you can shape; trust in the God who watches over you and all that you say and do . . . In Christ, you can believe in the future even though you cannot discern its shape. You can hand yourselves over to the Lord of the future, and thus overcome your discouragement at the magnitude of the task and the price to be paid . . . so do not be afraid to commit your lives to peace and justice, for you know that the Lord is with you in all your ways. [Pope John Paul II, Message for World Day of Peace, 1 January 1985]

PEACE AND YOUTH

This challenge to peace is specially calculated to inspire young people. To today's young people I should like to say that young men and women all over the world are rejecting the false romanticism of war and are campaigning for peace. They are protesting against weapons of war, especially nuclear armaments. They are struggling against the injustices that breed war, but they are pursuing justice through the way of non-violence. The youth of Ireland must become part of this worldwide movement and must apply its spirit and its methods to our conflict here in the North. Young people must not let themselves be misled by the propaganda of violence. They must not confuse the legitimate and necessary struggle for justice with a campaign of physical force.

I am much heartened by the magnificent response of our young people to the invitation of Pope John Paul: 'I appeal to you to use every means to forge new bonds of peace in fraternal solidarity with young people everywhere' (Pope John Paul II, Message for World Day of Peace, 1 January 1987).

Peace for the future is, in an important way, in the hands of our young people; I have complete confidence that you will accept that responsibility and be worthy of that trust. I am confident that Catholic young people will, as the Pope requests, use every means and every occasion to forge new bonds of peace in fraternal solidarity with young people of other religious communions and different political views, so that a truly new Ireland can be born in the peace of Christ.

The building of peace must be a gradual, patient and persevering task, to be taken up anew day after day. It will not be an easy task or quickly accomplished. But the builders of peace can take to themselves the words of Julian of Norwich:

> He said not:
> 'Thou shalt not be tempested;
> Thou shalt not be travailed;
> Thou shalt not be distressed.'
> But He said:
> 'Thou shalt not be *overcome*.'

We pray the old Irish prayer:

> The peace of the Father of good fortune,
> The peace of Christ in his passion,
> The peace of the Spirit of graces,
> Be with us and with the young generation.
> [Padraig Ó Fiannachta, *Saltair, Prayers from the Irish Tradition*, English translation by Desmond Forristal, Columba Press, Dublin, 1988]

# 11
## CHRISTIAN HOPE

*I came here to proclaim peace and love, to speak to you about the Son of God made man, about your life in Christ. Yes, as successor of the Apostle Peter I came to confirm my brethren in the faith, and to ask all Ireland to lift up its heart to a new vision of hope – in the words of St Paul: to 'Christ Jesus our hope' (1 Timothy 1: 1).* [Pope John Paul II, Address at Shannon, 1 October 1979; in *The Pope in Ireland*, p. 83]

A dangerous mood of hopelessness seems to threaten many in Northern Ireland at present. Many are finding it hard to believe any longer in a better future, a future of peace, justice and reconciliation. Even those who speak and work for peace and justice find it difficult to maintain their enthusiasm and their hope. It is hard not to feel at times that there is no use in speaking any more: everything has been said and there is nothing new to say. It is hard not to feel at times that there is no use in trying any more: everything has been tried and there is nothing new to try. Now surely is the time for the Churches to be heralds and sustainers of Christian hope.

Emmanuel Mounier said that 'the opposite of pessimism is not optimism but hope'; he defined hope as 'an indefinable meaning of simplicity, of pity, of stubbornness and of grace'. The search for peace and justice in Northern Ireland requires a faith-filled stubbornness. It does not look for easy or quick results. It refuses ever to admit defeat. It knows that, as Abbot Vonier once said, 'Christ has won all our battles for us long before we were born.'

It calls for the kind of hope of which St Paul spoke:

All of us who possess the first-fruits of the Spirit, we too groan inwardly as we wait for our bodies to be set free. For we must be content to hope that we shall be saved – our salvation is not in sight, we should not have to be hoping for it if it were – but, as I say, we must hope to be saved since we are not saved yet – it is something we must wait for with patience. [Romans 8: 23–25]

225

But the hope must be rooted in reality, not wafted aloft on pious rhetoric or sentimental gesture. We must keep trying – trying everything that holds promise of promoting trust, tolerance, mutual understanding, or of advancing even a little towards justice, reconciliation and peace. The unattainability of the best must not be an excuse for not doing the present and attainable good. As Pope John Paul said in Drogheda, we must 'attempt the seemingly impossible to put an end to the intolerable' (*The Pope in Ireland*, p. 22).

GRADUALISM

Micro-realisations of hope are preferable to no realisations. Our motto must be *nihil intentatum pro Christo; nihil intentatum pro caritate Christi.* We must leave nothing untried for Christ, nothing unattempted for his love. The solidarity in faith and hope and prayer of our brothers and sisters in Christ in other countries is a great comfort and strength. We thank them for it. We ask them please to continue to help us in prayer and in Christian love.

All political parties must accept the law of gradualism. Change of political and social structures is a necessary condition of that justice that is the essential precondition of peace. The necessity for such change and the cost of such change were reflected in *Populorum Progressio*, in which Pope Paul VI said, 'The present situation must be faced with courage and the injustices linked with it must be fought against and overcome. Development demands bold transformations, changes in relations that go deep. Urgent reforms should be undertaken without delay' (p. 32). Some speak of radical overthrow of the whole existing order, followed by a revolutionary reconstruction of society. Revolutionaries have only contempt for reforms, which they dismiss scornfully as 'bourgeois reformism'. They regard normality as a danger and normalisation as a threat to the revolution.

But revolution itself must inevitably be followed by a prolonged series of reforms, designed gradually to bring about a more just and equal society. Armed revolution only makes those reforms more difficult, more fragile, and especially more costly in terms of human suffering and damage to human rights and human dignity. The great Medellin document of the Latin American bishops says, '[The Christian] knows that sudden and violent changes of structures would be deceptive and ineffective in themselves and certainly not agreeing with the dignity of the people.' The way of peaceful reform is gradual; but this gradualism is the condition of that spirit of peace that alone can keep justice from destroying itself. What Raymond Williams called 'the long revolution' is a more efficacious way to justice than is violent revolution. Above all, it is the Christian way.

People in both communities must be prepared to acknowledge and to welcome reforms, even when they do not yet go the whole way to meeting their demands. To take one example, nationalists should be ready to acknowledge gradual reforms, when and in so far as they occur, in the administration of justice, in the impartiality of the police, in the operation of government services, in fair employment, in the economic rehabilitation of deprived areas. Such acknowledgement of progress, where it occurs, will be not only deserved and due but also an encouragement to further reforms, and will lend more credibility to criticisms of the slowness of reform when these criticisms are deserved.

To acknowledge the undoubted efforts the RUC have made, for example, will both indicate to them that they are making advances in the right direction, and will also signal to them that they still have a great task before them, to repair historic distrust and to make themselves accepted, as they clearly wish to be accepted, as a professional force impartially serving both communities.

Concretely, nationalists and Catholics should acknowledge progress in impartial policing by readiness to join the RUC and see this as service to the whole community. One condition for the acceptability of the RUC by Catholics and nationalists as an impartial, professional law-enforcement body is its reflecting in

227

its membership a balanced representation of both Northern Ireland communities.

It is also important that each community should welcome reforms that are justly sought by the other community. It is further necessary, and it is a Christian duty, that everyone should contribute, according to his or her opportunity and capacity, to the work of reform. Pope Paul VI, in the passage from which I quoted above, went on:

> It is for each one to take his share in [these reforms] with generosity, particularly those whose education, position and opportunities afford them wide scope for action ... In so doing, they will live up to men's expectations and be faithful to the spirit of God, since 'the ferment of the Gospel rouses in man's heart a demand for dignity that cannot be stifled'. [*Populorum Progressio*, p. 32; the final quotation is from Pope John XXIII's encyclical *Mater et Magistra*]

NON-VIOLENCE

Reform is the name for peaceful revolution, which is ultimately the true and Christian form of revolution and which is a condition for justice. Let me refer to two great modern champions of the Christian and non-violent way to justice, Helder Camara of Brazil and Oscar Romero of El Salvador. Both of them lived in societies afflicted by gross injustices and glaring inequalities, in which the poor were oppressed by 'national security' regimes of appalling brutality and ruthlessness. Yet both remained committed, in spite of everything, to the way of non-violence and to the revolution of love.

Archbishop Helder Camara said in his celebrated book *Spiral of Violence:*

> If violence is met by violence, the world will fall into a spiral of violence ... the only true answer to violence is to have the courage to face the injustices which constitute violence ... Common sense obliges one to choose between bloody and armed violence, on the one hand, and on the other the violence of the peaceful, liberating moral pressure ...

You think perhaps that only armed violence will have the power to shake and demolish the inhuman structures which create slaves. If I joyfully spend the rest of my life, of my powers, of my energies in demanding justice, but without hatred, without armed violence, through liberating moral pressure, through truth and love, it is because I am convinced that only love is constructive and strong. [*Spiral of Violence*, Sheed and Ward, London, 1971, pp. 55, 82]

Archbishop Oscar Romero said:

From the experience of history, we know how cruel and painful is the price of blood and how hard to repair are the social and economic damages of war. [James R. Brookman, *Oscar Romero, Bishop and Martyr*, Sheed and Ward, London, 1982, p. 173]

Archbishop Romero died as a martyr to justice and non-violence. His episcopal motto was '*Sentir con la Iglesia*', 'To be of one mind and heart with the Church'. The words serve now as the epitaph on his tombstone. Let this be the motto for us all: to be of one mind and heart with Pope John Paul in his repeated pleas and prayers for peace and justice, through the ways of non-violence, in the world and in Ireland.

POLITICAL LOVE

Our love for God and for others is the result of God's love for us, and must therefore reflect God's love. For the Christian, this love must determine all our attitudes, emotions, judgements, relationships: in our individual, family and professional lives, but also in our communal and political lives. Love must inform our politics as well as our personal behaviour, if we are to be truly Christian. Love is the first political imperative for the Christian.

To be genuinely Christian, this love must always be first to take initiatives, ready to take risks, prepared for rebuff and refusal. In unforgettable terms, St Paul describes Christian love as 'always patient and kind . . . never rude or selfish; it does not take offence and is not resentful . . . it is always ready to excuse, to trust, to hope and to endure whatever comes' (1 Corinthians 13: 4–7). How radically our situation in Northern

Ireland would be transformed if we really applied the norm of Christian love to our political behaviour. The Christian cannot wait for 'the others' to love first; he or she must be first to love. The Christian cannot wait for 'the others' to make the first move; it is the Christian who must make the first move. The Christian cannot demand that 'the others' change first before loving them; 'the others' can be changed only by our loving them first as they are. The Christian cannot lay down preconditions for loving others or make exceptions or exclude certain groups or communities. Like God's love for us, our love for others must be unconditional. We must not demand that others be our friends before loving them. We must love our enemies, even while they are still hostile. The Lord's words are quite categorical; there is no place to hide from His challenge as it is presented to us by His beloved disciple St John:

> Let us love one another
> since love comes from God . . .
> Anyone who fails to love can never have known God,
> because God is love . . .
> this is the love I mean:
> not our love for God,
> but God's love for us when He sent His son
> to be the sacrifice that takes our sins away . . .
> We are to love, then,
> because He loved us first.
> [1 John 4: 7,10,19]

Christ's commandment of love is new because, like God's love for us, it always makes the first move. It always takes the initiative. It goes out to the unloved and the unlovable, and makes them lovable and loved by first loving them as they are. God's love does not wait until we are His friends. It is His love which makes us His friends. St Paul says that God loved us and reconciled us with Himself through His Son 'while we were still enemies' (Romans 5: 10). God's love does not wait for our response: our response is the result of His love for us; our love for Him and for others is the first gift of His love to us. God's love does not even wait for us to change and repent

230

before He forgives us: we are able to change and repent because He has already forgiven us in Christ. Our repentance is simply our acceptance of the forgiveness He offers us; it is our accepting the reconciliation He has already brought about for us through Christ. We never love God first; He always loves us first; our love for God and for others is simply our loving and thank-filled recognition that we are loved by Him.

THE CHRISTIAN REVOLUTION

Jesus says:

> I say this to you: love your enemies and pray for those who persecute you; in this way, you will be sons and daughters of your Father in heaven, for He causes His sun to rise on the bad as well as on the good . . . if you love those who love you, what right have you to claim any credit? . . . if you save your greetings for your brothers, are you doing anything exceptional? Even the pagans do as much, do they not? You must therefore be perfect, just as your heavenly Father is perfect. [Matthew 5: 44–8]

I am afraid that we Christians have often tamed and privatised and diluted these words, as we have done with other words from the lips of Christ. We have called them counsels of perfection, thereby subtly satisfying ourselves that they are meant for exceptional elite groups in the Church, but not for 'ordinary Christians' like ourselves. But Christ is here stating basic elementary Christian precepts, meant for all Christians. They are the actual identification marks of the followers of Christ. Christ said: 'By this love you have for one another, everyone will know that you are my disciples' (John 13: 35).

We must try to realise again how radical, how revolutionary, Christianity is. We must see afresh what a radical transformation it has to make in our lives, what a revolution it is meant to create in our society. The Christian, every Christian, is called to be a revolutionary, but a revolutionary of love. For ourselves and for our society Christianity is nothing less than a new creation, a new social order, a new heaven and a new earth. It means a death to old or ordinary ways of thinking and behaving, and rising to a new life in Christ. It means putting on 'the new self, that has been created in God's way' (Ephesians 4: 24). It means having in us 'the same mind that was also in Christ Jesus' (Philippians 2: 5). St Paul says firmly:

> I . . . urge you in the name of the Lord, not to go on living the aimless kind of life that pagans live . . . Now that is hardly the way you have learnt from Christ, unless you failed to hear him properly when you were taught what the truth is in Jesus. You must give up your old way of life; you must put aside your old self . . . Your mind must be renewed by a spiritual revolution. [Ephesians 4: 17, 20–3]

CHRIST IS OUR PEACE

Before such a radical challenge we might well feel discouraged. But let us never forget Christ's words: 'For men, this is impossible; but not for God. All things are possible for God' (Matthew 19: 26). It is God who acts; we only allow Him to act in us. It is God who saves; we accept Him as Saviour. It is always God who loves first, loving us and enabling us to love others by letting His love flow out through us to them. Pope John Paul II said in his peace message for New Year's Day 1988:

> As the People of the New Covenant, we know that our freedom finds its highest expression in total acceptance of the divine call to salvation, and with the Apostle John we profess: 'we know and believe the love God has for us' (1 John 4: 16), the love manifested in His Word made flesh. From this free and liberating act of faith there flows a new vision of the world, a new approach to our brethren, a new way of existing as a leaven in society. It is the 'new commandment' (John 13: 34) which the Lord has given us; it is 'his peace' (John 14: 27) – not the peace of the world that is always imperfect – which he has left us . . . We have to commit ourselves with all our strength to living the new commandment, allowing ourselves to be enlightened by the peace which has been given to us and radiating it to those around us.

Also let us never suppose that God's kingdom of justice, love and peace exists only outside time and space and beyond history. It is true that the full manifestation and actualisation of the kingdom take place at Christ's Second Coming. But the kingdom is also already here. It is a reality in our world. It is the mightiest power in our society and in our world. The kingdom is very near to us. It is in the midst of us (Luke 17: 21). The kingdom is Christ in us, Christ amongst us, Christ in all the death-defeating power of his love, in the full victory and glory of his resurrection. In Christ, love *has* triumphed. No hate can finally prevail against it. God's love has the first word in creation and in salvation. Love, through Him, will have the last word in human history. We Christians are the people 'who have known and put our faith in God's love towards ourselves' (1 John 4: 16).

Let us look at the example of Mary, the first disciple, the first Christian. She knew and put her whole faith in God's love towards His people. She lived by faith in God's Word; she kept that Word and pondered it in her heart (Luke 2: 19, 51). Mary's whole existence was a receiving of God's all powerful Word into her life, first into her heart and mind and will through faith, and then into her womb as Word made flesh to dwell amongst us. She believed that God's Word could and would do what it promised. She was blessed because she 'believed that the promise made her by the Lord would be fulfilled' (Luke 1: 45). Mary said: 'I am the handmaid of the Lord; let it be done to me according to your word' (Luke 1: 37–8). Blessed are we if we believe as Mary believed, if we hope as Mary hoped, if we love as Mary loved. Blessed are we and blessed shall our society be if we never cease to put our faith in love.

At a time that is marked by anxiety and suspense but full of potential for great hope of a new future in peace and reconstruction, may all Christians, Protestant and Catholic, deserve the commendation of St Paul, that we

have shown our faith in action,
worked for love, and persevered through hope,
in our Lord Jesus Christ.
[1 Thessalonians 1: 2–3]

# 12

## PEACE: A GIFT OF GOD, A HUMAN TASK

*To pray is to be reconciled with him whom we invoke, whom
we meet, who makes us live. To experience prayer is to accept
the grace which changes us; the Spirit, united to our spirit,
commits us to conform our life with the Word of God. To pray
is to enter into the action of God upon history: he, the sovereign
actor of history, has wished to make people his collaborators.*
[Pope John Paul II, Message for World Day of Peace, 1 January 1984]

Peace is a gift that only God can give and that must be implored
from God in intense and persevering prayer; peace is also a
task for us men and women to undertake untiringly. Prayer for
peace and work for peace are inseparable from one another
and are in a sense the interior and the exterior of one single
reality.

THE WORK OF GOD

Sometimes we contrast work and prayer; there are times when
we actually seem to put more faith in our own work than in
prayer. We speak of turning to prayer as though this were a last
and desperate resort, to be tried when everything men and
women can do has failed. We find ourselves saying things like,
'There is nothing left but prayer.' Sometimes it seems to be
with an air of fatalism and almost despair that we say, 'It's all
in God's hands now'; and this is not far from meaning 'There
is no hope.' All this is wrong. It is a sad caricature of prayer. A
deeper understanding will show that prayer is the greatest power
on earth, because it is an effectuation of God's almighty power;
this deeper reflection will show that prayer is infallibly answered,
by uniting us with God in love and power.

Prayer is God working in us. We are conscious of the effort
needed in order to pray – the effort to attend to the presence of
God, the effort to concentrate, the effort to be still, to be
sincere with God. Awareness of our effort could deceive us
into thinking that prayer is our doing. We feel that when we

pray we are doing something for God, giving something to God. In fact, prayer is something God is doing for us, something God is giving to us. Prayer is what we receive from God, before it is our asking God for what we hope to receive. Prayer is a gift from God to us. The first thing we should pray for is to be given by God the grace to pray; for the grace of prayer is the basis of all the other gifts we hope to receive from God. The first thing we should give thanks to God for when we pray is for the grace of prayer itself. The fact that we can pray is itself an answer to prayer; for prayer puts us in touch with God; prayer gives us union with God in love; prayer makes us receivers of God's love. When we pray, God's infinite power becomes His total loving attention to us, here, now. God's greatest gift to man is Himself, and prayer infallibly gives us God, unites us with God. Consequently, there is no such thing as unanswered prayer. Every prayer is answered: God is the answer. What else do we desire, whom else do we need, but God? As St Teresa put it:

> He that has God is lacking in nothing.
> Only God is enough.

Prayer is therefore the most powerful force we can bring to bear on any situation. Prayer, indeed, is the power of God working through us in a given situation. When we pray, we are letting God create and transform ourselves first, and then the world through us. When we pray, God is allowing us to share in His own power. He is making us co-operators in His own work.

PRAYER AND CREATION

One great manifestation of God's power and work is the creation of the world. The world exists because God is causing it to exist. It is not just that God created the world long ago in the remotest past. God is creating the world now, in every instant of its existence. As long as the world is, the world depends for every atom of being that it has totally on God as its continuously all-powerful and all-loving cause. God is at every moment of time loving the world into existence. He is simply loving the world to be. Prayer is God letting us share in His causing of the world. Prayer is our taking to ourselves the share God offers us of responsibility for the world. The seventeenth-century French religious thinker Blaise Pascal said that God established prayer 'to communicate to His creatures the dignity of causality' and also 'to teach us from where our virtue comes' and 'to make us deserve other virtues by work' (*Pensées*, no. 513).

It is false to contrast prayer and work. We do not fall back on prayer as a last resort when all else has failed. As St Ignatius Loyola and other saints have put it, we must pray as if everything depended on God, and work as if everything depended on ourselves. The motto of the early and medieval monks was '*laborare et orare*', to work and to pray; these two were inseparable. Prayer gives us a sense of responsibility before God and with God for the state of the world. Prayer makes us conscious of God's will and purpose for the world. In the prayer that Jesus taught us, we say, 'Thy will be done on earth as it is in heaven'. As we pray these words, we realise that God's will is not being done on earth as long as there is war, violence, murder, abortion, crime, injustice, oppression, racism, discrimination, denial of human rights and human dignity. We cannot pray these words of the Lord's Prayer sincerely unless we are doing everything we can to resist and remedy these evils and to bring the world closer to the direction of God's will and purpose. We cannot consistently pray to God unless we are also working with Him to have His will done in the world of men and to construct an earthly kingdom that will be in the pattern of His heavenly kingdom.

PRAYER THROUGH JESUS CHRIST OUR LORD

Prayer shares in the mighty power by which God created the world. It also shares in the still mightier power by which God redeems and renews and re-creates the world through the coming of Christ and through the Passion, death and resurrection of Christ. God's greatest gift to us is Himself. He gives Himself to us through giving us His Son. Our Lord Himself said to Nicodemus:

> God loved the world so much
> that he gave His only Son,
> so that everyone who believes in Him
> may not be lost
> but may have eternal life.
> [John 3: 16]

A greater gift than the gift of His Son God cannot give. Jesus Christ is the final answer given by God to all men's questionings and longings, all men's aspirations and hopes, all men's desires and needs and prayers. St Paul says that Jesus Christ is the 'Amen' that God says to us at the end of all our prayers. 'Amen' means 'yes', 'May it be so', 'Let the prayer be answered' (see 2 Corinthians 1: 20). As St Paul puts it, it is God who says the Amen, not we. We say the prayer, God says the Amen. We express our petition, we expose our need, and God says: 'your prayer is answered', 'it is so as you desire'. The answer God gives is Christ himself, God's gift to us. Christ is God's complete answer to all our prayers, all our desires, all our needs. Christ is the total fulfilment by God of all His promises to mankind. We must remember that in the New Testament, in the Book of the Apocalypse, Christ is himself called 'the Amen' (Apocalypse 3: 14).

All this St Paul expresses in the words: 'However many the promises God made, the Yes to them all is in [Christ]. That is why it is "through him" that we answer Amen to the praise of God' (see 2 Corinthians 1: 20-1). Once again, we see that there is no such thing as unanswered prayer. Every prayer is answered: Christ is the answer. Whom else do we need? We do not have to 'wait for someone else' (Luke 7: 19). Only Christ is enough.

Christ's own most intense and anguished prayer was the prayer poured out from his agonised heart in the Garden of Gethsemane and from his parched throat on the Cross: yet humanly speaking it seemed unanswered prayer. In the garden,

240

he prayed, 'Father, if you are willing, take this cup away from me' (Luke 22: 42). Two days later he was to drink the bitter cup of crucifixion, crying out from the Cross, 'My God, my God, why have you deserted me?' (Matthew 27: 46). Yet this supreme prayer of Jesus Christ received from the Father the answer that alone fulfils all mankind's longing, answers all humanity's prayers and meets the deepest needs of the human heart – the resurrection of Jesus from the dead, the coming of the Holy Spirit, the gift of the Church, the Eucharist, the sacraments, the forgiveness of sins and our hope of resurrection and everlasting life. It is in and through that apparently unanswered prayer of Jesus that all our prayers are answered.

IN THE HOLY SPIRIT

If Christ is God's greatest gift to us, then Christ is also our greatest return gift to the Father. Christ himself is our most powerful and irresistible prayer to the Father. This is another reason why we end our prayers 'through Jesus Christ Our Lord'. The words imply that in our prayer we are offering Jesus Christ back to the Father, who first gave Jesus Christ to us. Our prayer is Jesus Christ praying for us to the Father, praying in us to the Father, giving to his Father through us praise and thanks and glory 'as it was in the beginning, is now and ever shall be'.

Jesus' prayer to the Father in us expresses his loving union with the Father through the Holy Spirit, who is the love of Father and Son. Since our prayer is Jesus praying in us, our prayer unites us too in love with the Father through the Holy Spirit of love. Every prayer we say gives us the gift of the Holy Spirit. This is the explanation of a lesson on prayer that Jesus gives us in the Gospels. His words are quoted by both St Matthew and St Luke, but with an important difference. In both Gospels, we have Our Lord teaching us that prayer cannot fail to be answered. He says:

> Ask, and it will be given to you; search, and you will find; knock, and the door will be opened to you. For the one who asks always receives; the one who searches always finds; the

241

one who knocks will always have the door opened to him. [Matthew 7: 7–8]

To reinforce the lesson, Our Lord uses an analogy. He asks:

> Is there a man among you who would hand his son a stone when he asked for bread? Or would hand him a snake when he asked for a fish? If you, then, who are evil, know how to give your children what is good, how much more will your Father in heaven give good things to those who ask him? [Matthew 7: 9–11]

St Luke quotes the words of Our Lord exactly as St Matthew does, but introduces an important variation at the end. He records Our Lord as saying:

> If you then, who are evil, know how to give your children what is good, how much more will the heavenly Father give the Holy Spirit to those who ask him! [Luke 11: 12–13]

The meaning is clear. The Holy Spirit is the best of all the 'good things' God gives to men and women in answer to their prayers. The Holy Spirit is the answer God gives to all our prayers. Every prayer gives us the Holy Spirit, uniting us in Jesus Christ to the Father. There is no such thing as unanswered prayer. Every prayer is answered: the Holy Spirit is the answer. To speak of unanswered prayer would be almost like the response some poorly instructed disciples gave to Paul at Ephesus. Paul asked: 'Did you receive the Holy Spirit when you became believers?' They replied: 'No, we were never even told there was such a thing as a Holy Spirit' (Acts 19: 2).

Prayer is the presence and power in us of Almighty God, the Father, the Son and the Holy Spirit. Prayer is our letting the most blessed and adorable Trinity, the thrice-holy and most strong triune God, *be God* in us. It is letting God be Creator God, Redeemer and Reconciler God, Sanctifier God, in us; and be so through us in our world. That is why all prayer is heard; because God answers it by giving us union with His triune self. This is why all prayer is efficacious; because it releases God's almighty power. This is why no prayer is ineffectual, all prayer is powerful: its power is the very power of

God. Its work is the work of God. For centuries, the prayer of the Church in monasteries has been called 'the *Opus Dei,* the work of God'. It is both the work of God in us and through us in the world; and also our most important work for God. The word 'liturgy' is derived from Greek roots meaning 'the work of God's people'.

PRAYER, PASSION, RESURRECTION

We pray through Jesus Christ. Our prayer is a sharing in the prayer of Jesus Christ. It is Jesus Christ praying in us. Jesus' supreme prayer was his prayer on the Cross. This was the only prayer ever uttered from this earth which deserved in its own right to be heard by the eternal Father; and it was heard on our behalf. The Letter to the Hebrews says:

> During his life on earth, [Christ] offered up prayer and entreaty, aloud and in silent tears, to the One who had the power to save him out of death, and he submitted so humbly that his prayer was heard. [Hebrews 5: 7]

All the power of Christ's prayer on the Cross, all the love and all the potency of Christ's Passion, are placed behind our prayer, which is offered in the name of Jesus Christ.

God gave a sign, gave proof, that Christ's prayer was answered. The sign was the resurrection of Jesus from the dead. The power of God, invoked by the dying prayer of Jesus, raised Jesus from the dead and exalted him on high, above 'all beings in the heavens, on earth and in the underworld' (Philippians 2: 9–10). All the mighty power God exerted in the resurrection and ascension of Jesus Christ and in the sending of the Holy Spirit is behind our prayer when we pray in the name of Jesus; and all Christian prayer is prayer in the name of Jesus; and Mass, which re-presents to the Father the Passion, death and resurrection of Jesus, is the greatest Christian prayer.

PRAYER, RECONCILIATION AND FORGIVENESS

We can never say that prayer for peace is ineffectual; any lack in its effectiveness can lie only on our side, in our lack of faith and trust, sincerity and perseverance. We can never say that prayer for peace is an escape from work for peace. The work of peace is being performed in and around us by God's power even as we pray for peace. We are being brought into closer union with God as we pray, and we are therefore being drawn into closer union with all those whom God loves. We cannot be sincere in our prayer to God unless, while praising and loving Him, we are also honouring and respecting His image reflected in the men and women He has made in His own image and likeness.

We cannot be sincere in our prayer unless were are praying to become forgiving persons ourselves. When we pray as Jesus himself taught us to pray, we ask that God may forgive us our trespasses, for we recognise that we are sinners in need of God's forgiveness; but we make the granting of our own very request conditional upon our being ready to forgive those who trespass against us. Indeed, more accurate translation makes it clear that we make it conditional upon our *having first forgiven* those who trespass against us. We pray to be forgiven; but, as a prior condition of this, we pray to be forgivers. As we pray for peace, we are being drawn into oneness with Jesus Christ and our prayer is, in fact, Jesus Christ praying in us. Our prayer therefore, if it is genuine, must include the prayer of Jesus himself on the Cross for those who were persecuting him: 'Father forgive them.' Jesus' supreme prayer was his death of love for those vowed to enmity against him. If we are praying sincerely, we must share in Jesus' spirit of forgiveness. Jesus' supreme work was the work of reconciling men with God and with one another. When we pray, we are letting his work of reconciliation be done in us; we are letting his spirit of reconciliation be operative in us.

The Birmingham Six found in prayer the way to survive their long ordeal of unjust imprisonment with their integrity as persons intact and their inner peace undisturbed. Dick McIlkenny calls prayer *'the pathway to peace'*. He speaks of how for the first four years of his imprisonment he felt bitter and angry and did not pray. Then he came to see that bitterness and anger were simply destroying him as a person and he began to try to pray again. It was difficult at first and he nearly gave up the effort. Slowly but gradually prayer became less of a struggle and more of a joy and eventually became a natural part of daily life, as necessary as eating or sleeping and even more satisfying. With prayer, he rediscovered forgiveness and release from anger, and with this the peace that the world cannot give and that nothing can take away, peace within himself, peace with God, peace with others, peace even with those who had so cruelly wronged him and the other five innocent prisoners. Billy Power has had the same experience of finding through prayer the exorcism of the self-poisoning venom of hate and anger and thereby attaining a peace beyond understanding.

Prayer is not only an appeal for the spirit and work of reconciliation; it is the work of reconciliation already in progress. By praying for peace, we are all sharing in the 'ministry of reconciliation' of which St Paul speaks:

> It is all God's work. It was God who reconciled us to Himself through Christ and gave us the work of handing on this reconciliation. In other words, God in Christ was reconciling the world to Himself, not holding men's faults against them, and He has entrusted to us the news that they are reconciled. So we are ambassadors for Christ; it is as though God were appealing through us, and the appeal that we make in Christ's name is: Be reconciled to God. [2 Corinthians 5: 18–20]

When Churchmen talk about the Northern Ireland problem, they are sometimes accused by politicians and others of being remote from the hard realities of life, the harsh choices that politicians must confront, the constraints imposed by the real upon the possible. They are criticised as soft-centred sentimentalists. They are made to appear naive and preachy.

It is true that when Christians speak of love and reconciliation they can appear sentimentalist and impractical. An English critic once said impatiently, 'The person who says that all the world's problems could be solved by love is bluntly a fool.' But this is a critique of an emasculated understanding of love, far different from love as the Christian Gospel understands it. Christian love is not weak and generalised benevolence. It is strong, it is costing in that it is a challenge to revolution, the true and lasting revolution that changes hearts and minds and as a consequence fearlessly accepts the need to change structures and institutions. It is dynamic. It is a force for change. It is a call to conversion. St Paul says, 'Your minds must be renewed by a spiritual revolution' (Ephesians 4: 22).

Reconciliation, which is close kin to love, is not an emotional experience, not even a purely spiritual state. It is not simply a reaching out in love of person to person. It is also a reaching out of community to community. It involves the dismantling of structures that alienate communities and exclude persons and classes from their fair share of society's resources. It involves the replacement of these structures by institutions and policies that enhance the sense of belonging of individuals to communities and of communities to one another, and which respect human rights and human dignity and promote personal growth. To choose love does not mean deciding that nobody must get hurt. It means, instead, deciding and accepting and persuading others to accept whatever hurt and sacrifice through loss of privilege one person or group must accept, in order that another person or group may have simple justice. Christian love *most certainly is* the only final answer to Northern Ireland's problems. But this must and will entail hurt and sacrifice and costing change on the part of both communities. It shall and it must require political change.

POLITICS AND THE CHRISTIAN GOSPEL

Politics is indeed an arena of vital concern for the Christian. Christ's kingdom 'is not of this world', but it has immediate and imperative consequences for the behaviour of men and women in this world and for the way in which they organise their corporate living and structure their society. Karl Barth spoke for all the Churches when he declared that every Christian sermon must be in some sense political.

Nevertheless the translation of the standards of the kingdom

of God into specific political programmes and the application
of the Gospel to concrete social situations are matters in which
there can be legitimate variety of opinion between members of
the Church. These are matters for debate and personal decision
by Christian lay men and women. It is not within the competence or authority of the Church's pastors to prescribe or to
forbid specific party political choices, so long as these do not
conflict with God's Commandments. The pastor's task is to
proclaim the Gospel and to alert consciences to the moral and
social implications of the Gospel, its bearing on human rights
and on social justice, its consequences for relationships between individuals, communities and classes in society. But the
Church cannot allow the Gospel to be confused with any party
political programme or annexed by any political party. This
would turn the Gospel into an ideology. It would make the
Gospel the slave of a man-made institution instead of a force
for liberation of the human spirit from all merely human and
temporal systems. The Vatican Council declared in its Pastoral
Constitution on the Church in the Modern World:

> It is of supreme importance, especially in a pluralistic society, to
> work out a proper vision of the relationship between the political
> community and the Church, and to distinguish clearly between
> the activities of Christians, acting individually or collectively in
> their own name as citizens guided by the dictates of a Christian
> conscience, and their activity acting along with their pastors in
> the name of the Church.
> The Church, by reason of her role and competence, is not
> identified with any political community nor bound by ties to any
> political system. It is at once the sign and the safeguard of the
> transcendental dimension of the human person . . . [The Church]
> never places its hope in any privileges accorded to it by civil
> authority . . . But at all times and in all places the Church
> should have true freedom to preach the faith, to proclaim its
> teaching about society, to carry out its task among men and
> women without hindrance, and to pass moral judgements even
> in matters relating to politics, whenever the fundamental rights
> of man or the salvation of souls requires it. In so doing, she
> may use only those means which accord with the Gospel and

247

with the general welfare as it changes according to time and circumstance. [*Gaudium et Spes*, no. 76]

The Vatican Council insists that political activity falls essentially within the responsibility and competence of the laity. They must be 'guided by the light of the Gospel and the mind of the Church, and prompted by Christian love', but in their task of renewing the temporal order the laity act 'in a direct way and in their own specific manner' (cited from Decree on the Apostolate of Lay People, Vatican II, *Apostolicam actuositatem*, 18 November 1965, no. 7; and from *Christifideles Laici*, 30 December 1988, nos. 42–3).

### THE IRISH CHURCHES

To find the right relationship between the Christian faith and political action, or between the Church and the State, is one of the great and recurring tasks of the Church in every age. It is a great preoccupation for the Catholic Church in Ireland, and it is a particularly delicate task for Churchmen in Northern Ireland at this time. It is for the good of both religion and of politics that the spheres of both be clearly distinguished. Churchmen in our divided society must not speak only to or for one political community. They must as far as possible speak across the community divisions, having in mind at all times the reactions of the other community, their rights, their fears and hopes, their sensitivities. To win the respect of both nationalist and unionist communities is, it seems to me, part of what it means to be a minister of reconciliation in our country today.

The Churches must give leadership. They cannot and must not act as spokespersons for political parties or as proxies for political leaders. They can and they must lead only by the standards of the Gospel, taking their stand on the Gospel values of inter-community reconciliation, mutual forgiveness, the pursuit of peace through justice for both communities, shared concern for the rights of both communities, and especially for the poor, the deprived, the homeless, the badly housed and the unemployed in all sections of society.

Churchmen must work, together, if possible, to calm the

atmosphere and promote a climate of reconciliation. They should do everything possible to encourage people to give quiet, reflective and prayerful consideration to the paramount need for reconciliation and reconstruction of the fractured social fabric and the vulnerable economy of our land.

Reconciliation must at all times be a priority concern for all the Churches. The Inter-Church Working Party that in 1976 produced the report to the Churches entitled *Violence in Ireland* declared:

> We suggest that the direct application of the ideal of reconciliation to our present predicament includes:
>
> (i) That all political leaders should be encouraged to see their task as that of reaching a just agreement with their opponents rather than of achieving victory over them; and that to this end they should be open to any reasonable settlement proposed.
>
> (ii) That all people of goodwill should use their votes and their influence to encourage the politicians to see things that way . . .
>
> (v) That in every possible way . . . and remembering that joint action is in itself a source of enhanced mutual knowledge and understanding, the Churches and their members should *act together* in support of the call made together by their leaders *to talk, to think, to pray peace.* [pp. 88–9]

The words are more starkly relevant now than when they were first uttered.

THE BRITISH CHURCHES

The British Churches too have an important role to play. The most important help the British Churches can give is of course their prayer. Prayer is the greatest power at the disposal of Christians. I know that the conflict in Ireland features frequently in the prayers of the Churches in Britain.

The Churches can work also to dispel the simplistic assumptions and inherited prejudices about Ireland that are sometimes to be found in Great Britain, and to promote greater understanding of the Irish situation and especially of the complex problems of Northern Ireland. In particular they can seek to promote greater acceptance among the British public of the fact that these problems are a residual consequence of Britain's colonial history in Ireland and are a continuing responsibility for the British government and people. The Churches can seek to dispel hand-washing dismissals of the problem as though it were due only to peculiarly Irish perversities. The joint programme for education in justice and peace worked out by the Irish Council of Churches and the Irish Catholic Bishops' Justice and Peace Commission might serve as a useful model for an educational programme in British as well as in Irish schools.

The Churches could endeavour to encourage balanced treatment and in-depth analysis in the media of the Irish problem, penetrating beyond the ugly scenes of violence to the underlying causes. In particular, they should protest against the anti-Irish reporting and feature-writing in some of the mass-circulation British newspapers, which often take on a nasty racist tinge. The Churches in Britain should be concerned about abuses in the operation of the Prevention of Terrorism Act and about the welfare of Irish prisoners in British jails. In particular, they could keep pressing for a re-examination of the cases of Mrs Annie Maguire and her friends and the late Giuseppe Conlon, who from the beginning never ceased to protest their innocence, and about whose trial and sentences the gravest doubts persist.

The Churches in Britain should try to understand and to promote understanding of the feelings and fears of the unionist community, and not leave people content to react with disgust and disdain against the uglier manifestations of those feelings. They should try also to understand the feeling of alienation and injustice which a long and bitter history and continuing experience have caused in the nationalist community.

FAITH, LOVE AND HOPE

In 1985 an inter-Church group published a discussion document entitled *Breaking Down the Enmity*. As its authors say, the document has a particular value because it was 'the work of a group of Protestants and Roman Catholics, Northerners and Southerners, struggling together with the issues of faith and politics in Ireland today, and the relationship between them'. Among the authors were several leading Protestant clergy from Northern Ireland. The document concludes:

> Political structures will not of themselves end the conflict, but they may provide a context in which respect between the two communities and between Britain and Ireland might slowly grow again and in which enmity might gradually be turned into friendship. Churches are called to be a Sign of the Kingdom of God, a Kingdom in which fear and enmity are overcome. We in the Churches are called to this task today in Northern Ireland, Britain and the Republic. It is our submission that being a Sign of the Kingdom means in part that we work for new political structures in Northern Ireland in which the identity of both Nationalists and Unionists is respected and in which neither one can dominate the other.

Let no Christian ever say that the task is hopeless. The Christian is above all a man or woman of hope. G.K. Chesterton said:

> As long as matters are really hopeful, hope is mere flattery or platitude. It is only when everything is hopeless that hope begins to be a strength at all. Like all Christian virtues it is as unreasonable as it is indispensable.

## ONLY GOD IS ENOUGH

We who believe in Christ's peace and who try to live by Christ's law of love are men and women of boundless and indomitable hope. To God, nothing is impossible. With Christ, all things are possible. St Teresa of Avila said:

> Let nothing disturb you.
> Let nothing frighten you.
> All things pass;
> God does not change.
> Patient endurance overcomes everything.
> If you have God, nothing is lacking to you.
> If you have not God, nothing will satisfy you.
> Only God is enough.